MW00966298

To: Crystal,
Blessings to You!

JEREMY J. ANDERSON

STRENGTH & CONDITIONING

SPIRIT REIGN
PUBLISHING
A Division of Spirit Reign Communications

Spirit Reign Communications
P.O. Box 322
Capshaw, AL 35742
256-759-7492
www.spiritreign.org

Author: Jeremy J. Anderson
Cover design: Ornan Anthony of OA.Blueprints, LLC
Page design & layout: Ornan Anthony of OA.Blueprints, LLC
Editor: Spring Hawk Publications

Scripture quotations marked KJV, are from the Holy Bible King James Version.
Scripture quotations marked NIV, are from the Holy Bible New International Version.
Scripture quotations marked NLT, are from the Holy Bible New Living Translation
Scripture quotations marked ESV, are from the Holy Bible English Standard Version.
Scripture quotations marked NLV, are from the Holy Bible New Life Version.
All definitions are from the Websters Dictionary.

Printed in the United States of America

ISBN Hardback: 978-1-940002-19-4
ISBN ePDF: 978-1-940002-20-0
ISBN ePUB: 978-1-940002-21-7

STRENGTH & CONDITIONING

CONTENTS

DEDICATION

I dedicate this book to my Grandmother,
the late Patricia Ann McCormick.

ACKNOWLEDGMENTS

I want to first thank my God for the *Strength & Conditioning* training I receive from You daily. With you I am stronger.

Special Thanks to my gorgeous and amazing wife Traci & our precious daughter Jewel. Special thanks to all the participants in my focus group: Edwin McBride, Tawanna Anderson, James Brandon, Alexis Lawrence, Bryan Cordell, Monode Desrosiers, Dr. Katie Arnette, Mason West III and Stephanie Rox-Strong.

To Ryan & Charisse Felton, Jason Bulgin, Jon Johnson, Seth & Holly Yelorda, Micha Logan, and Jaspertena Stewart. Thank you for opening your hearts and sharing your stories. Your contribution gave life to this book.

To Eric Hickman and the Viridiun Foundation, thank you for your continual support in the ministry God has set before us.

Thanks to Javan Cornelius and Shoeshine Media for the video series.

INTRODUCTION

Are you a real Christian? I ask because many people today have a distorted view of what real Christianity and Discipleship mean. Many are unaware that there's a distinct difference between "believing" in Christ and actually "following" Him. Believing in something doesn't necessarily mean you're a part of it. God isn't looking for people to just believe in Him or His church; He's looking for us to become a part of His church. *The Modern Disciple Series* will give you a clear picture of what a true Christian and Disciple of Christ should be. The premise of my ministry has been to help the lukewarm church turn up the heat. It gives me great joy to help people transition from being a believer in God to becoming an actual follower of God.

It's clear in Luke 9:23 that there are three things that we must do in order to be a true disciple (Christian). Those three things are: Deny yourself, pick up your cross daily, and follow Jesus. In *Self-Destruction*, the first book of this series, I focused on the first step to true discipleship, which is denial of self. This book *Strength and Conditioning* will show you, the average Christian, how to pick up your cross daily. I called Volume two of this series, *Strength and Conditioning*, because I believe God allows trials to come our way so we can find our strength in Him as He conditions us for the kingdom of heaven.

Strength & Conditioning is written from a fitness perspective so we can view the "crosses" that we bear as a way of getting spiritually fit. So often we view the trials of life as either a punishment from God or an attack from Satan. Rarely, if ever, do we count it all joy, as James suggests in James 1:2-4: *"My brethren, count it all joy when you fall into various trials, knowing that the testing of your faith produces patience. But let patience have its perfect work, that you may be perfect and complete, lacking nothing."* We'll address the question—why bad things happen to good people, and get a deeper sense of why God allows the trials of life as training for our spiritual growth.

According to Webster's Word Histories, a derivative of the adjective gymnos, the Greek gymnasion, became the Latin *gymnasium*, which was used in two distinct senses to mean both "an exercise ground" and "a public school." So, I invite you into God's Gymnasium where the pain will result in great gain. The word *pain* or some form of it appears in the Bible over 70 times. The word is first used to explain the pain of childbirth: *To the woman He said, 'I will greatly multiply your pain in childbirth, in pain you will bring forth children; yet your desire will be for your husband, and he will rule over you' (Genesis 3:16, NASB)*. Here in Genesis we see that when Adam and Eve sinned, the pain of childbirth was one of the consequences of their sin. The ground was cursed also because of their sin and, as a result, death entered into the world. Pain, we now know, is one of the byproducts of the original sin.

Each chapter of this book adopts the character of fitness training. Within each chapter you'll be strengthened & conditioned by the understanding of God's word. At the end of each chapter, you'll hear from real people who have had to carry their crosses, but you'll also hear how the experiences of those crosses strengthened their walk with God. In addition to the personal stories, I filmed a video series to accompany each chapter. You can view the videos on my website www.jeremyanderson.org or scan the QR code provided and watch from your smartphone or tablet. This book is also great for small groups, so you may use the space at the end of each chapter called - "Basic Training" for notes. Also, enjoy the Group Training Study at the end of the book for further study.

Enjoy your workout!

SCAN THE QR CODE

TO WATCH THE CHAPTER VIDEO FOR EACH CHAPTER.

It's simple and easy to use from your Smartphone or Tablet!

Enjoy a special video from Jeremy for each Chapter of this book.

You can also enjoy the videos from our website, www.jeremyanderson.org

"Scan the QR Code to view the video for the chapter, or visit our website www.jeremyanderson.org."

Chapter 1

THE GYM MEMBERSHIP

Fitness gyms across the world have their highest peak of new memberships in January. Why, you ask? This peak in enrollment is due to the millions of New Years' resolutions people make. Most of these fitness commitments are from people deciding to make a physical change in their lives. Some want to get in shape, lose weight or gain more muscle, while others just want to live a healthier lifestyle. Regardless of their motivation, one thing is for sure, they all see the benefits of joining a gym.

I've had several gym memberships in my day so I can testify to the benefits of joining a gym. I even have a fitness center set up in my home, but it's not the same as working out with other people. There's something special about walking into a fitness gym and seeing people of all ages and walks of life grinding, sweating and growing physically. The people you workout with, in a sense, become your accountability partners. It's exhilarating and refreshing, well...maybe not refreshing due to all those people sweating, but the scene of a fitness gym

{ JESUS PAID OUR MEMBERSHIP FEES WITH HIS SHED BLOOD. }

definitely gets your blood pumping!

In this chapter we'll discuss the correlation between the body of Christ (God's church), and a fitness gym. One provides you spiritual growth while the other promotes physical growth. Throughout this book, when I'm referencing the "Church," I'm not necessarily talking about a building, but rather a group of people who believe and follow Christ. Most fitness gyms you join require you to sign a 1 or 2 year contract. When we sign up for Gods church, He gives us a lifetime membership. We've actually had this membership all along, we just needed to claim it. Just as there are costs for a gym membership, there are costs when you join the body of Christ; the only difference is Jesus paid our membership fees with His shed blood. The membership in God's church puts us in a position to grow spiritually with Him.

Please don't mistake my point—just because the membership is free doesn't mean you don't have to do your part. Faith is nice but if your faith or membership lacks works on your part it won't work. This is why the Bible says, 'faith without works is dead.' People don't lose weight by just signing up to the gym, the true transformation in their lives takes place when they put in the work at the gym! When you combine faith and works in your relationship with Christ, you gain real spiritual growth.

INVESTING IN YOUR TRANSFORMATION

I'll never forget the $1,200 investment I made into Gold's Gym. It was my junior year in college and I decided I was going to get fit. I wanted to gain more muscles and have abs of steel. Unfortunately, my transformation never materialized. I got the workout gear, running shoes and fancy membership but none of it was enough because I never used it. That's right, $1,200 down the drain. You see, being tied to God's church and having a membership isn't enough. You have to make the investment by being active so you can reap the full benefits of the membership. You can be a member of a fitness gym, have all the right clothes and even show up but never change. The same is true with God's church. You can show up at church on weekends wearing nice suits, dresses, shiny shoes, all the right attire, but still never change. Scary thought isn't it? Christianity takes time, energy and effort. Just as you invest and join a gym with some sort of transformation in mind, the same applies to God's church. You joined God's church and became a Christian with the hope of being transformed daily.

At the end of the day, people join fitness gyms because they want to see change. It should be the same thing in God's church. The whole point of joining God's church and claiming Christianity is to accept Jesus Christ as your personal Savior. Accepting Christ isn't enough. True acceptance, leads to conviction and conviction leads to change. When you

ACCEPTING CHRIST ISN'T ENOUGH. TRUE ACCEPTANCE, LEADS TO CONVICTION AND CONVICTION LEADS TO CHANGE.

accept Christ, what you're really saying is that you're ready to go through the process of being changed. This is the part that a lot of people struggle with. Change can be a very painful yet necessary process. Just as the body builder experiences pain during his training so does the Christian who's growing in Christ.

Recently, I was leaving my gym and in passing I spoke to a friend of mine. I inquired about his experience with his personal trainer. His first response to me was *"it's rough, I didn't know what I was signing up for."* I laughed, then encouraged him not to give up. I even think I told him I could see some changes. I hope I wasn't lying? I wonder how many Christians feel the same way my friend felt about his training regimen. You see, no one told him how painful and rough the physical training would be. I've yet to meet someone who by joining the gym alone began to lose weight. Signing up for the membership is all well and good, but what you invest in is what brings about real transformation.

THE STRUGGLE

Many times we sign up for the membership because we see buff, fit and muscular people, but we don't see their struggle. We're impressed by the size of the gym and the equipment, but rarely do

GOD DESIRES US TO BE SPIRITUALLY CONDITIONED FOR THE KINGDOM OF HEAVEN.

we focus on the process of physical fitness and growth. It's the same with the church. We see the people who are in the big beautiful churches so close and connected to God. We think all we have to do is join this big pretty church and our life will be perfect. Wrong! What we don't see is the behind-the-scenes footage of their spiritual growth!

Romans 8:17 (NIV): Now if we are children, then we are heirs—heirs of God and co-heirs with Christ, if indeed we share in his sufferings in order that we may also share in his glory.

Here in Romans, Paul is saying that since we're heirs of God, and co-heirs with Christ then we will share in His sufferings and glory. Many preachers today are missing the mark when they call people to give their lives to God. We tell them the good but don't tell them the struggle. We've been known to paint pictures of a perfect, stress-free life. That's not biblical! When you sign up for a membership in the body of Christ, you're signing up to become spiritually fit. When I joined my gym here in Huntsville, AL, I had an ultimate goal of where I wanted to be physically. When I joined God's church I had an ultimate goal of where I wanted to be spiritually. God desires us to be spiritually conditioned for the kingdom of heaven.

WE SHOULD VIEW THE CHURCH AS A HUGE FITNESS CENTER.

John 14:1-2 (NKJV) "Let not your heart be troubled; you believe in God, believe also in me. In My Father's house are many mansions; if it were not so, I would have told you. I go to prepare a place for you."

The Bible makes it plain that Jesus left and has prepared a place for you. There's a place for us in heaven that God is preparing for us now! Since we have a membership and we are children of the King, we have an inheritance in God's kingdom. In order for us to become inhabitants of our inheritance we must not only have a membership in God's church, but we should also be members of God's body. The process isn't easy which is why we must learn to embrace the struggle that comes along with the membership.

BENEFITS OF A MEMBERSHIP

As I stated before, I have a fitness center in my house, but it's not the same as having my gym membership. When I arrive at the gym at five a.m., I see the same familiar faces every day. It's also encouraging to be around others who are growing as I am. That's the biggest benefit to having a membership—being in an environment full of regular people like yourself who are also striving to reach their physical goals.

The same is with God's church. It is not His will for us to grow by ourselves spiritually; the very groundwork of the church was formed to encourage spiritual fellowship. We should view the church as a huge fitness center, full of different parts in the body of Christ. The Apostle Paul discusses this in the first book of Corinthians.

1 Corinthians 12:12-14 (NIV) "Just as a body, though one, has many parts, but all its many parts form one body, so it is with Christ. For we were all baptized by one Spirit so as to form one body whether Jews or Gentiles, slave or free and we were all given the one spirit to drink. Even so the body is not made up of one part but of many."

We see here that God's body is made up of several parts, and every part has equal importance. Many churches today don't grow as they should because certain parts of the body (members) aren't working together. Notice how Paul addresses this problem:

I Corinthians 12:21-27 (NIV) "The eye cannot say to the hand, "I don't need you!" And the head cannot say to the feet, "I don't need you!" On the contrary, those parts of the body that seem to be weaker are indispensable, and the parts that we think are less honorable we treat with special honor. And the parts that are unpresentable are treated with special modesty, while our presentable parts need no special treatment. But God

BE PREPARED FOR DAILY TRIALS AND PERSECUTION.

has put the body together, giving greater honor to the parts that lacked it, so that there should be no division in the body, but that its parts should have equal concern for each other. If one part suffers, every part suffers with it; if one part is honored, every part rejoices with it. Now you are the body of Christ, and each one of you is a part of it."

Satan's main point of attack is to divide and conquer. He tries his best to separate us from the fold because he knows how powerful and spiritually encouraging the other parts of God's body can be. I am physically at my best when I'm consistent in the gym. Sometimes due to my travel schedule, I'll workout at home or in the hotel fitness centers but it isn't the same. There's something special about being in the gym working out and growing with the other members.

A CHURCH THAT SUFFERS

Be prepared to suffer. That's right, it's part of the process of spiritual growth. Jesus made it very clear in Luke 9:23; He told his disciples that they would have to carry their crosses daily. In other words, be prepared for daily trials and persecution! Just as Christ suffered, there's a level of pain and suffering that we'll have to endure also. I know that sounds blunt and harsh but it's the truth. If your pastor bap-

YOU CAN BE IN THE CHURCH BUT NOT OF THE CHURCH.

tized you and said, *"Welcome to a perfect life,"* then let me be the first to apologize for the misconception. Peter warned us of the sufferings we'll experience:

I Peter 4:12-13 (NIV) "Dear friends, do not be surprised at the fiery ordeal that has come on you to test you, as though something strange were happening to you. But rejoice inasmuch as you participate in the sufferings of Christ, so that you may be overjoyed when his glory is revealed.

Did that verse just say rejoice in the participation of Christ's sufferings? It sure did. As a matter of fact, Peter said don't be shocked as though something strange is happening to you when you suffer. He also suggests that we should rejoice so that we can be overjoyed when His glory is revealed. Doesn't this sound strange? That's the kind of God we serve. I'm sure it seemed strange to the angels when Jesus left the glory of heaven to come to an earth full of wickedness to die for our sins.

I Peter 4:16 (NIV) "However, if you suffer as a Christian, do not be ashamed, but praise God that you bear that name."

Here's where it all makes sense to me. Due to sin and the corruption that's taking place in our world,

JESUS DIDN'T GO TO THE NEXT LEVEL UNTIL HIS PERSECUTION TOOK PLACE.

we will experience sufferings anyway. No one is exempt from sufferings, but my reality is different from non –believers. Since I know that our Redeemer is coming back soon to save us, I embrace my sufferings and the crosses I carry as strength and conditioning training. In biblical times and even today, you have people who were literally happy to die for God. Isn't that amazing? Their level of commitment was so serious they found it an honor to suffer for the one who suffered for them! I guarantee you one thing, this church that suffers today, won't suffer always. God is coming back for those who are members of His church. As we're getting spiritually fit, He's working on our characters through the trials we experience.

IN THE CHURCH BUT NOT OF THE CHURCH

We have a better understanding now of the value of a gym membership. We also see how important it is to be a member in God's gym, His church. We should also understand the importance of putting our memberships to use. Just showing up to the gym isn't enough, we have to allow the gym experience to change our lives. I guess what I'm saying is you can be in the church but not of the church.

Look at the Life of Judas Iscariot; he was one of Jesus' original disciples. Judas was in the church and studied under Jesus for three years. Now we're all familiar with the story of Judas and how he betrayed Jesus. I mention Judas because it's important for us to grasp the importance of being an active member of God's church, and allowing the experience and power of God to penetrate our souls. You see, Judas was a member in the flesh but not a member in the spirit. He showed up every weekend for service, but he wasn't allowing the very presence of God to change his heart.

Here's an interesting thought: When Christ called Judas to follow Him, He already knew Judas would betray Him. Think about it, God is all knowing. So you may ask yourself why Jesus would call a man to follow Him if He knew this man would ultimately betray Him? Well, the simplest answer is that He loved Judas. Jesus didn't force Judas to love him. Judas' betrayal was part of the plan. Jesus didn't go to the next level until His persecution took place. The same is with you, there are certain levels that God wants to take you to and the trials you endure often times build the bridge to that place. In this book we'll highlight the necessity and benefits of our trials.

Have you ever wondered why Jesus clarified to His disciples what it *really* took to be His disciples? Why would He tell His disciples what it meant to be a *disciple*, if they were already disciples? You see, Judas carried the name "disciple" but was he really a disciple? In Luke 9:22, Jesus was letting His disciples know that He was about to suffer many things and would experience rejection. Then in verse 23, He told them the three things needed to be His *true* disciples. In other words, Christ was saying, if you're really about me and my work then you'll be able to accept these three requirements: deny yourself, pick up your cross and follow me.

Judas had a membership but never used it. He traveled with Jesus, ate with Jesus, saw miracles performed by Jesus but he never experienced Jesus. Jesus is calling us all to have an experience with Him. Jesus is calling us to move past the realm of being pew warmers to experience a real, true and intimate relationship with Him. He does warn us though that with this intimacy comes a price. Throughout the next few chapters we will see how this intimate, yet painful, process is actually a purification process preparing us for our prize above.

My Workout Plan

My strength and conditioning workout plan was the first of many. For years I would read the story of Judas and would fume with anger. How could he betray my Christ? How could Judas betray Jesus for thirty pieces of silver? How could he spend so much time around The Savior and not be changed? I got a better understanding of Judas when I took my eyes off of him and placed them on myself.

As I began to examine my personal life I noticed that Judas and I had a lot in common. My father and grandfather were preachers. I was raised in a Christian home—even put in Christian schools. In my high school years, I was chaplain in my senior class and religious vice-president. I was a naturally-talented young leader, but things in my life began to change. I became like Judas and betrayed God for my thirty pieces of silver. When I got to college my life shifted from being about God to being about me.

I was going to church every weekend but I wasn't a part of the body. I would hear the sermon with my ears but my heart wasn't receiving it. My cold heart had nothing to do with the church building or members. My rebellion was not a result of the music or the sermons. My reason for being lukewarm was that I wasn't willing to surrender my life to Christ. You see Luke 9:24 says, *"For whoever wants to save their life will lose it, but whoever loses their life for me will save it."* I simply wasn't willing to give up my life totally to God.

Honestly, at that time my heart was so cold I wasn't even thinking of being a disciple for Christ. I was chasing money, women, cars and popularity, yet I still had a membership. When I say I had a membership, I mean, I was still professing to be a Christian. Christianity isn't about what you believe, it's about what you do! Do you see why having a membership to God's church is important but what's even more important is being an active member?

It wasn't until I hit rock bottom that I was able to hear the voice of the Lord. The same way I would shake my head in shame at Judas, I was years later doing the very same thing. I sold God out for luxury cars, two nightclubs and lots of drugs. Here's the sad part, during this time in my life I was still going to church! I would run the streets at night, go the church the next day, and then throw a party at my club that same night. I was in the church but not of the church.

God is a God of love. Soon this lifestyle started to come to an end. The doors to my sinful operation began to close. He knew that as long as I was *on top of the world*, I would never come to Him, so He allowed my little world to crash. After the dust settled and depression fell upon me, He whispered to me "*your membership is still valid*." Wait, what? You mean to tell me after all of these years of crime, drug dealing, drug abuse and fornication, you still want me? Not only was God saying that He still wanted me, He also made it known that He still wanted to use me. It was at this time that my relationship with Christ became real.

It was in this moment that I looked at my membership to God's gym as a true training ground. This was one of the roughest transitions of my life. Hitting rock bottom was a painful and humbling process, but a necessary one. God knew exactly what He was doing. What I experienced from my membership with God and His church has made me into the God-fearing man I am today. I can truly say that there is salvation in God's gym.

Basic Training

1. Why should we view God's church as a fitness center?

2. How can someone be "in" God's church but not "of" God's church?

3. Why did Romans chapter 8 say we would share in Christ's sufferings?

4. Why does Peter tell us in 1st Peter chapter 4 to rejoice in sufferings?

5. What does Judas and many so-called Christians today have in common?

6. What, if anything, have you been selling God out for?

THE GYM MEMBERSHIP

"Scan the QR Code to view the video for the chapter, or visit our website www.jeremyanderson.org."

Chapter 2

YOUR PERSONAL TRAINER

Any real fitness center will have personal trainers. Most personal trainers had to go through special training to become certified. One of the first questions a personal trainer will ask you is: "Why did you join the gym and what results are you looking for?" They ask this because they need to know what you're expecting to gain from their training program. Once the trainer has an understanding of what you're looking for, they then put together a comprehensive workout specifically designed for you. There isn't a one-size-fits-all approach when it comes to a person's physical growth. A good personal trainer will know which workout plan is best for you, and what it takes to help you meet your physical goals.

About a year before I began writing this book I was going through a very troubling time. My normal sense of comfort was being challenged and I didn't like it. Frustrated and discouraged, I asked God what the reason was for my pain. God clearly told me He was trying to get me conditioned for

> **THOUGH GROWTH IS A PAINFUL PROCESS, THE PROCESS IS NECESSARY.**

the kingdom of heaven and that what I was going through was conditioning me for the next level of my ministry. God knew exactly what I needed to go through to get to that next level in my spiritual life.

This is where I came to know Jesus as my personal trainer. It made so much sense to me. Just like a personal trainer coaches their clients to physical fitness, Jesus was coaching me to spiritual fitness. Though growth is a painful process, the process is necessary. Right before this trying time I remember specifically asking God to take me to the next level. I felt like I was at a comfortable place in my life and ministry, which was fine, but I knew that God had more in store for me. God had given me visions and dreams of where I'd be in ministry; I just didn't know what the process of getting there would be. The interesting thing about personal trainers is they're not necessarily concerned with how much pain you endure, their main responsibility is to get you in shape. Around this time in my life, Jesus was asking me if I wanted to be comfortable or if I wanted to grow.

IT'S ALL GOOD

Here's a fact: Nothing catches God by surprise. God's not sitting in heaven saying, "Man, I didn't see that one coming. Ok, let's make a plan to fix this." No way! Our God is a sovereign and perfect God who is very intentional. He doesn't make bad things happen to us but since He is all-powerful, one would say that He allows it. Our God isn't a dictator either, which is why He's given us all free will to make our own decisions. Sometimes regardless of the decisions we make, He will allow bad things to happen that will work out for our good in the end. With this in mind, I have a deeper appreciation for the Bible when it confirms that everything happens for a reason.

Romans 8:28 (NIV): "And we know that in all things God works for the good of those who love him, who have been called according to his purpose."

Whenever a trial comes, a family member dies or someone loses a job, Romans 8:28 is the most chosen verse that Christians share. Often times when this verse is used it leaves the recipient confused and mad at God. What's meant to be offered as words of comfort is often received as a one-size-fits-all answer. You're basically telling that person, not to worry, you getting cancer is part of God's plan. To those of us Christians who lean on Romans 8:28, let's make sure we use it on ourselves when trying times come our way. I believe in what Paul says here in Romans, the question is, 'can we say this to ourselves and find true comfort within this scripture?'

WE MAY NOT ALWAYS UNDERSTAND THE PROCESS BUT WE MUST TRUST THE PROCESS.

Is it true that God's in control? Yes. Does God want His children to get cancer? Of course not, but God is so amazing that He can make the cancer work to your benefit. It's not possible to live in a perfect world because of sin. So God takes an imperfect world and makes His perfect will in our lives work out for our good. God is our personal trainer, so we may not always understand the process but we must trust the process. Remember, Jesus, our personal trainer is responsible for getting us to that next level spiritually. He seeks to strengthen our faith and condition us for heaven. Let's be honest, our characters are far from perfect. If Jesus were to come now, the iniquity found in our hearts would prohibit us from entering the Kingdom of heaven. The suffering and trials we endure actually help us persevere and build stronger character.

Romans 5:3-4 (NIV): "Not only so, but we also glory in our sufferings, because we know that suffering produces perseverance; perseverance, character; and character, hope.

Paul here in Romans stresses the importance of finding glory in our sufferings. Now you're probably wondering how we're able to find glory in our sufferings. I wondered the same thing. When you're working out, lifting weights and you feel that burn, you know your muscles are growing and you're getting stronger. Jesus as your personal trainer will strengthen you spiritually. The verse in Romans also says that our sufferings produce perseverance, and that our perseverance produces character, and that our character produces hope. The key is for us to view our struggles and challenges in a way that we know they'll eventually make us better and stronger.

THE PERFECT PLAN

What if I told you that your siblings would kidnap you and sell you into slavery? What if I told you that after that, God allowed you to go to prison even though you we're innocent? Then what if I told you those experiences would condition you to be the vice-president of the United States. Well that's similar to the workout plan God designed for Joseph. God's goal was to prepare Joseph for something great, but he had to be strengthened and conditioned.

Let's take a look at the workout plan God put together for Joseph. Joseph was the beloved son of Jacob and was loved dearly by his father. Jacob's favoritism toward Joseph caused his half brothers to hate him. What made matters worse is that Joseph told his brothers two dreams God had given him that implied the family would one day bow down to Joseph. Think for a moment about the dreams, visions or promises that God has given you. Now ask yourself if you're prepared to go through the work-out plan designated for those dreams to come to life?

Joseph's brothers plotted to kill him, however, the eldest brother, Reuben, didn't want Joseph to die. They decided to sell Joseph for twenty pieces of silver to a caravan of Ishmaelites, and told their father, Jacob, that Joseph was killed by a wild beast. Imagine the mental torture Joseph was going through. Kidnapped by his brothers, then sold as a slave to strangers. I wonder if Joseph was questioning the workout plan God was putting together for him.

Proverbs 3:5-6 (NIV): "Trust in the Lord with all your heart and lean not on your own understanding; in all your ways submit to him, and he will make your paths straight."

We're all familiar with what Proverbs says, and many of us have been reciting this verse most of our lives. This is one of those classic scriptures you learn as a child but do you believe it? Let me tell you why I ask that. Joseph was kidnapped by his brothers and then sold as a slave. I wonder what state of mind young Joseph was in during this time. Joseph had to get to the point where he moved past his own understanding and trusted in God.

Joseph was eventually sold as a slave to Potiphar, the captain of Pharaoh's army. While serving in

GOD WILL ALLOW YOU TO PROSPER EVEN DURING PERSECUTION AND PAIN.

Potiphar's household, the Bible states that God was with Joseph and, because of that, he prospered in everything he did. This tells me that God will allow you to prosper even during persecution and pain. You see, God is with all of us no matter what we're going through. Joseph soon found favor with Potiphar and became his personal servant and was eventually promoted to oversee Potiphar's entire household. After his promotion Potiphar's wife sought to have an affair with Joseph. Potiphar's wife was persistent in her pursuit of Joseph but he refused to have sex with her for fear of sinning against God. Let's be clear here, Joseph didn't refuse to sleep with Potiphar's wife because she wasn't attractive, nor did he decline the sexual gesture for fear of Potiphar. Joseph didn't sleep with Potiphar's wife because he didn't want to sin against God.

Embarrassed and mad that Joseph constantly refused her advances, she made a false accusation against him by claiming he tried to rape her. This resulted in Joseph being thrown into prison. How would you feel doing the right thing only to be punished for it? At any time, Joseph could have given in and slept with Potiphar's wife but Joseph wouldn't sin against God. You see, Joseph was in covenant with his personal trainer.

A DREAM COME TRUE

To make a long story short, Joseph was called from prison to interpret the dreams of Pharaoh. The dreams that Joseph interpreted saved Egypt from the soon coming famine. As a result of this, Pharaoh released Joseph from prison and placed him in charge of all the land of Egypt. This story is concluded by the famine reaching Canaan, which put Joseph's brothers in a position where they had to get clearance from him to get food. Just like in Joseph's dream—they bowed before him.

Jeremiah 29:11 (NIV): "For I know the plans I have for you," declares the Lord, "plans to prosper you and not to harm you, plans to give you hope and a future."

Here the Bible says that God, our personal trainer knows exactly what He has planned for our lives. The hope and future He wants us to experience doesn't come without sacrifice. The frustration and pain that Joseph endured was training for something greater. Before God could bless Joseph with that power he had to do a work within his soul.

The story of Joseph is filled with drama and pain. Joseph was sold into slavery by his brothers, accused of a crime he didn't commit, and then left in prison for years. All the while, Joseph stayed faithful to God. God was Joseph's personal trainer, and was with him the whole time. Let's not forget that

THE MANIFESTATION OF OUR DREAMS COMING TRUE IS A PAINFUL PROCESS.

Genesis 39:2 says: God was with Joseph. The nature of a personal trainer is to stay with your trainee during the workout, and it's obvious God was with Joseph from the beginning. Joseph stayed faithful to God and eventually became the most powerful man in Egypt, second only to Pharaoh.

God has given us all dreams and aspirations. The fulfillment of those dreams will only come when the one who gave us the dreams takes the necessary steps to make them come true. Sometimes the manifestation of our dreams coming true is a painful process. It is when we awake from the journey that the nightmare becomes a dream come true. The same was with Joseph. His dreams turned into a nightmare when his brothers kidnapped him and sold him into slavery. But he was eventually exalted and they all bowed before him.

Each level that Joseph reached was achieved by passing a specific test. You see, God always had it planned for Joseph to be second in command of Egypt, but before he could promote him there, Joseph had to be strengthened and conditioned for that task. The process was frustrating and painful but necessary for true growth. Joseph didn't understand why he was going through these rough years

DON'T ALLOW YOUR LACK OF UNDERSTANDING TO DERAIL YOUR FAITH.

but God knew. Don't allow your lack of understanding to derail your faith.

Philippians 4:7 (NIV): "And the peace of God, which transcends all understanding, will guard your hearts and your minds in Christ Jesus."

Joseph had to adopt the peace of God since there was a lack of understanding. From the moment Joseph was kidnapped by his brothers, God was training him to be in charge of Egypt. As true disciples we must learn to hold on to our dreams. Sometimes all we have to hold on to during the workout process are the dreams that God has given us. These dreams will comfort us in times of need. Some of the very dreams God gives us will only be manifested during trying times. It's in those times that God has ordained a workout plan for our spiritual growth.

Jon's Workout Plan

Meet my friend Jonathan. His strength and conditioning workout plan was frustrating yet necessary. I've known Jon for about 14 years, and we have several things in common; we both love and have raised American Bulldogs, we both love basketball, and both our fathers are Pastors. Our families and fathers are also very close. I feel Jon's story is appropriate for the end of this chapter because, like Joseph, Jon also had a dream. God gave him a call to ministry years ago but it didn't come right away. As a matter of fact, it came when Jon felt it was the wrong time.

In 2008, Jon was living in Huntsville, Alabama, working a great job and got married to his wife, Alinka. After their marriage, Jon and Alinka got more serious about God. The Lord soon led them to an exciting new church family where they felt welcomed and loved. Within a year they were leaders and extremely active in their church. As their activity grew they found themselves taking more time for service and less time to do the things they normally did. The Lord was blessing Jon and Alinka so much that they both had great careers and bought their first house together. Sounds like the American dream, right? They had the education, the careers, the marriage, new house and now the church.

Jon and Alinka were experiencing some good times. Knowing the dreams and plans God had given Jon, he was reluctant to go when God called him to ministry. He and his wife were both settled in their careers, had just bought a home and were active in church, but God wanted more. Jon obviously had questions: When should he start this ministry? What areas would he minister in? And where should he minister?

Since Jon wasn't quick to make a move into ministry God gave him a nudge or two. In 2009, after being married for a year, Jon lost his job. On top of that his home was robbed several times. While all of this was taking place, Alinka became pregnant. Imagine the weight on Jon's shoulders; you and your wife are expecting a baby, you don't have a job and your home is repeatedly burglarized. Though he was confused, frustrated and felt forsaken, Jon kept the faith.

These unfortunate events gave Jon and his family the motivation to move to Atlanta, Georgia, to pursue his call to ministry and start their lives over. Jon had some opportunities lined up that looked promising and he really felt God was about to bless him and spark his ministry in Atlanta. The move from Huntsville to Atlanta was a challenge because they weren't able to sell their house. Eventually, they were able to move because they found a renter for the house in Huntsville. When Jon got to Atlanta he discovered that the ministry opportunity had fallen through. So Jon spent the next year looking for work in the Atlanta area.

For Jon and his family, 2010 was a rough year. They were living in Atlanta where the cost of living is somewhat higher than in Huntsville; their son was born and Jon still couldn't find a job anywhere. To make matters worse, the lady who was renting their house in Huntsville could no longer pay the rent so their house eventually went into foreclosure. You can imagine the state of depression my friend Jon was in.

Why was all of this happening? What was God doing in the life of my friend Jon? It appeared that Jon was doing everything right. He went to school, got educated, found a nice Christian woman, married her, saved their money, had good credit, bought a home and was active in church. Once they decided to pursue the ministry and fulfill the dreams God put within Jon, is when everything seemed to go wrong. They lost their jobs, their home, most of their savings, but didn't lose their faith.

The Lord eventually blessed Jon with a part time teaching job at a Christian Academy. He and his wife still struggled financially but they were making it. Feeling unfulfilled Jon questioned if he was even called to ministry in the first place. Things weren't working out at all how he planned. On top of the frustration he was feeling, his wife was expecting their second child. This pregnancy was extremely hard on Alinka. Jon wasn't getting benefits because he only taught part time, so that made their situation even more frustrating.

After an extremely difficult pregnancy their daughter was born. Now this young couple has two children and very little money. Every step of the way God was training Jon for something greater. Doors began to open up and Jon was allowed to teach more classes. Soon he got word that he was being considered for a full time position at another Christian academy. This news only served as torture to Jon's spirit after he found out he didn't get the position. He was hurt, tired, frustrated and unfulfilled, but Jon did not give up.

I think the thing that's most inspiring about Jon's story is his perseverance and faith in God. Just like Joseph, Jon knew that God had great plans for him. And like Joseph, Jon's good actions seemed to only slap him in the face. What God was doing in the life of Jon was getting his character in check. During this time Jon was traveling and doing seminars called "Character Construction"- the very thing God was doing in his own life. Jon continued to serve and gave his all to this part time job and his church. You can imagine Jon's prayer life going to a whole new level. You see, that's what trials do—they cause us to get real intimate with God. I've heard the most powerful and most sincere prayers come from the most broken hearts. Even though it seems as though God doesn't hear those prayers, He does.

I'm sure after Joseph interpreted the dreams of Pharaoh's baker & cupbearer and was still in prison for another 2 years, he wondered if God had heard his prayers. I believe that it's in those times when our faith and patience is tested that our blessings are activated. This waiting period that Jon was going through was just training. Jon losing his job, his house being robbed repeatedly, no work for over a year, his wife and the complicated pregnancies, and his house being foreclosed, were all tests and training.

Another struggling school year went by, and Jon and his family were still barely making it. After the summer, Jon got a call from a stranger about a possible job in Florida. Desperate for what God had in store for him, Jon traveled to Orlando Florida for the interview. By this time he and his wife were down to one car and that car was giving them problems. Their one car that worked broke down while Jon was in route to the interview. Not only did his car break down, but also when he got to the interview he found out he was up against other chaplains and pastors. It was clear that he wasn't nearly as qualified as the other candidates. How many of you know that if God has called you, you are more than qualified!

Due to Jon's diligence and constant pursuit of Jesus, God showed him favor. Jon got the job at a top Christian Academy in Orlando, FL. Jon was the school's new chaplain and Bible teacher! In addition to that, when the school found out about Jon needing transportation they gave him the keys to a Ford Expedition. Wow!

This whole time God was testing Jon's fortitude. God always wanted to bless Jon with the position he has now, but the training to be successful and trustworthy in this position was key. Just like Joseph, God gave Jon a vision and dream. They both had a calling on their lives and in their experiences, Jesus was able to play the role of "Personal trainer." Jesus was able to use the crosses they both carried to strengthen their faith and condition them for ministry.

Basic Training

1. Can you relate to Joseph's or Jon's story? If so, how?

2. Why does God use trials in our lives?

3. Based upon Romans 8, what advice could you give someone who is going through a rough time?

4. Ask yourself: Do you really believe in what Romans 8:28 says?

5. In Romans 5:3-4, why does Paul tell us to find glory in our sufferings?

6. How should we view our spiritual personal trainer?

7. What are the areas in your life where you feel like you could use a little spiritual strength training?

"Scan the QR Code to view the video for the chapter, or visit our website www.jeremyanderson.org."

Chapter 3

TRUSTING YOUR TRAINER

In chapter two, we discussed the importance of having a personal trainer. In this chapter we'll explore the importance of having a personal trainer that is both credible and trustworthy. Let's be honest, you want your trainer's body to show the signs of physical fitness. Now there's nothing wrong with having a trainer that has love handles, but if I were striving to have a six-pack and be in shape, I'd have more confidence in a trainer with a six-pack. A trainer's body should reflect what they're teaching and as a trainee, you want to know that they've experience what you're about to go through.

Why is it important that we trust our trainer, you ask? I'll tell you why. When you have a personal trainer pushing you to extreme levels physically, you want to be sure they know what they're doing. It's one thing to recommend something and it's another thing to have experienced what you're talking about. In addition to their body showing the physical evidence of their training, credibility is critical when looking for a trainer you can trust.

TRUSTING GOD IS KEY TO OUR SPIRITUAL GROWTH AND DEVELOPMENT.

It's the same with your spiritual walk. You have a trainer in Jesus, and his body has been proven to be worthy to give you the spiritual training you need. Just as you'd want the body of your personal trainer to reflect the training they've had, Jesus' body has the physical evidence to prove it. The physical evidence that you'll look for is in his hands. Who better to coach you and I through this spiritual walk and encourage us through the pain than someone who's had rusty nails driven through their hands and feet? There isn't a spiritual coach more conditioned than Jesus. Not only was He painfully beaten, ridiculed, and hung on a cross, but he also had the sins of the world on his heart. Here's the part that makes Him credible and trustworthy: He overcame it all!

John 16:33 (NIV): "I have told you these things, so that in me you may have peace. In this world you will have trouble. But take heart! I have overcome the world."

You see Jesus knows what it takes to live successfully here on earth. He also has a clear understanding of what betrayal and pain feels like from the sacrifice He made for our lives. Let's be clear, when we speak of "trusting your trainer" we're actually talking about having faith in Jesus. Remember that little thing that God said without which it's impossible to please Him? Yes, that thing. Trusting God is key to our spiritual growth and development. I believe that one of the main reasons God allows challenges and obstacles to come our way is to test our faith in Him. One of the jobs Christ has as our personal trainer is to strengthen our faith in Him.

COMPLAINING DURING THE WORKOUT

The first step in growing is a willingness to be trained. You must have faith in your trainer for them to get you where you want and need to be. One thing that can make the job of a personal trainer hard is someone who spends the whole workout session complaining, doing nothing and second-guessing the suggested workout regimen. Are you a complainer? Do you really trust God? Do you lose faith when the slightest thing goes wrong? I once heard that worrying and doubting are a sophisticated form of atheism. If you truly believe in God and trust in Him, why would you complain?

One of the worst things to see is a person saying that they can't do the workout. I know the workout can be hard but you've got to fight through. Any good personal trainer will stay with you the whole time during the workout. I've never seen a trainer tell a person to do a workout while they go and sip lemonade in the shade. You'll always find a good trainer in the gym right beside their trainee helping them along the way. That's how Jesus is with us; He'll

> **WORRYING AND DOUBTING ARE A SOPHISTICATED FORM OF ATHEISM.**

never leave us nor forsake us. Just because He's there doesn't mean the workout will be any easier.

SECOND GUESSING

Then there's the person who questions their personal trainer asking: "Why do we have to do crunches again? Can't we do another workout? I don't like doing squats maybe we should do something else." I've seen that when the person getting trained goes through a rough spot in their workout they begin to question and second-guess the trainer. It's the pain that makes us second-guess the one who's training us.

One day, while working out, I told a friend who was a trainer that we must be doing the workout wrong because of the pain I was feeling. He laughed and said, 'we were doing it right, I just wasn't used to working those muscles.' Just like my workout, God will change up situations in our lives so that He can work on areas that we normally don't work on. The question is: Do we trust the plan that God has in store for us?

Hebrews 11:6 (NIV): "And without faith it is impossible to please God, because anyone who comes to Him must believe that He exists and that He rewards those who earnestly seek him."

In the aforementioned verse in Hebrews, Paul makes two points. The first point is that you can't please God if you don't have faith in Him. That's what this whole chapter is about. The second point Paul makes is that, God rewards those who seriously seek Him. It's like the guy who goes faithfully to the gym five days a week; he will soon receive his reward, which is a fit and conditioned body. The same is true for the children of God. If we earnestly seek God and practice real, radical faith in our trainer, our reward will be a spiritually fit life. At times I have to move past the pain and focus on the trust I have in my trainer. Many times we go through hard times and the first thing we do is question or second-guess what God is doing. If you're like me, you've asked God these questions:

* Why would You allow this to happen?
* Why did You allow this to happen to me?
* Why did You let this happen the way it did?
* Why did You allow this to happen at his time?

{ OFTEN TIMES WHEN WE'RE FOCUSED ON THE PAIN OF THE WORKOUT, IT'S HARD TO ACCESS THE POWER. }

The discomfort of the trials often causes us to question God. What tends to happen is the focus that should be on God gets shifted to our pain. Our faith in God is where we get our power from that will help us deal with the pain we're battling. Often times when we're focused on the pain of the workout, it's hard to access the power. This power I'm speaking of comes from God but since we aren't disciplined our faith turns to fear. This is why God challenges us to operate outside of our comfort zone. We may not always understand the process but we must trust the process.

Isaiah 55:8-9 (NIV): "For my thoughts are not your thoughts, neither are your ways my ways," declares the Lord. "As the heavens are higher than the earth, so are my ways higher than your ways and my thoughts than your thoughts."

It's during the tests and trials of life that we have to believe that God is in control. This is the time when our love and faith in God is most showcased. We must believe that God knows exactly what we can handle and what we can't. His word says that He'll never give us more than we can bear right? WRONG!

GOD WILL GIVE YOU MORE THAN YOU CAN BEAR

I bet you weren't expecting that! Let's reason together. "God will never give you more than you can handle" is a phrase that's been preached, sung, written and recited for years. Doesn't that sound like the Gospel truth? It makes you feel good, secure, warm and fuzzy. Don't worry about the obstacles ahead of you! Your whole world may crash on top of you but don't worry, you got this!

GOD HAS TO GIVE YOU MORE THAN YOU CAN HANDLE BECAUSE IF NOT WE WOULDN'T NEED HIM.

Sorry, but this isn't biblical. It's time for us to move past the bumper sticker theology and see what God's really doing in our lives. God has a habit of giving people more than they can handle. To be frank, God has to give you more than you can handle because if not we wouldn't need Him. When you hear people say, "God will never give you more than you can bear," they're misquoting a line from I Corinthians chapter 10 where Paul is saying that we won't be tempted beyond what we can resist. Why? Because with every temptation God has built in a way of escape.

I Corinthians 10:13 (NIV): "No temptation has overtaken you except what is common to mankind. And God is faithful; he will not let you be tempted beyond what you can bear. But when you are tempted, he will also provide a way out so that you can endure it."

For years people have been misquoting I Corinthians 10:13. This says nothing about God not giving you more trials than you can handle. Some may interpret it as that but there's a clear difference between trials and temptation. The above text is stating that God won't allow you to be tempted more than you can handle, and that He'll give you a way of escape. It says nothing about God not giving you more trials than you can handle. What Paul says in the second book of Corinthians backs up my point that God will give us more than we can bear.

II Corinthians 1:8-9 (NIV): "We do not want you to be uninformed, brothers and sisters, about the troubles we experienced in the province of Asia. We were under great pressure, far beyond our ability to endure, so that we despaired of life itself. Indeed, we felt we had received the sentence of death. But this happened that we might not rely on ourselves but on God, who raises the dead."

When I read my Bible, I see many people who were given more trials than they could handle. Look at the lives of Job, Moses, Joshua, Mary, Paul, Elijah, Martha, or Jeremiah to name a few. These mighty men and women of God were only mighty because of the Mighty God they served. Their situations were the very thing that strengthened their faith in God. Each of them, at some point, had more than they could handle. I'm talking about lamenting, crying, groaning and even requesting that God take their lives. Now this doesn't sound like the cozy Christian life you've been hearing about, does it?

God knows that if He only gave us what we could handle, we'd have no need to depend on Him. The job of your personal trainer is to push you past your known limits. This is how you reach optimum growth. If our spiritual walk were up to us, we would stay in

> **IF GOD'S PLANS WERE RESTRICTED TO THE LIMITATIONS OF HUMANS HE'D NEVER GET ANYTHING DONE.**

our comfort zone and we wouldn't grow. I often find myself asking God to take my life and ministry to the next level. The reality here is that I'm dependent on Him to do what I can't do, therefore I need Him to give me something that I can't handle alone. God's plans for us are huge! If God's plans were restricted to the limitations of humans He'd never get anything done. God being the perfect God He is will give you and me way more than we can handle, which puts us in a position to lean on Him for strength. This is why the word of God says that 'we can do all things through Christ who gives us strength.'

FAITH ISN'T FAITH UNTIL IT'S TESTED

I was always intrigued by the story of Abraham. Here we have a 100-plus year old man who was promised by God that he would be the father of many nations. Genesis chapter 15 says that Abraham's descendants would be as numerous as the stars in the sky. Here's the problem: Abraham and Sarah were old, and In-vitro fertilization (IVF) wasn't an option. Here's the interesting thing, they trusted God enough to leave their home and land to come to Canaan but after 10 years, with no children, their faith in God was shaky.

Abraham didn't believe that God could bless his

ABRAHAM SAW HIS DESTINY IN HIS SON AND NOT IN HIS SAVIOR.

wife with a child due to their old age. Abraham, lacking faith decided to take matters into his own hands so they contrived a plan that involved Abraham sleeping with Sarah's servant Hagar. Hagar soon bore a son named Ishmael. The interesting thing here is that, God told Abraham that his seed would bear many nations. Abraham saw his destiny in his son and not in his Savior. That was the problem. Rather than keeping his covenant with God, trusting God to keep His word, Abraham decided to expedite things.

Enmity grew between Sarah and Hagar, so Sarah had Abraham send Hagar and Ishmael away. It had to be painful for Abraham to send his son away. As they left the land of Canaan, I imagine that Abraham struggled as he watched his destiny walk away. God is faithful even when we aren't. Years later, He gave Abraham and Sarah a son of their own. This was God's way of saying, "I told you so." By God allowing the seemingly impossible to happen, the faith of Sarah and Abraham increased. Sometimes God has to do the miraculous for us to see His hand in the situation.

Abraham was about to go to the next level with God, but there was a spiritual workout plan he had to go through first. He had sent his first son (born

> **YOUR COVENANT RELATIONSHIP WITH GOD IS TESTED THROUGH TRIALS.**

through Hagar) away, now God's request to Abraham was to sacrifice His son Isaac. You see, Abraham was in covenant with God. One thing I'm learning is that your covenant relationship with God is tested through trials.

Because of his lack of faith, God put Abraham in a position to increase his faith. God found something that Abraham dearly loved and made one simple request of him; give it to me. This request would prove to be a rough workout for Abraham. Imagine the agonizing pain that Abraham must have felt once he received the request from God. I'm sure Abraham had many of the same questions we have today: Why my son? Why now?

Now imagine the mental anguish Abraham had as he traveled for 3 days to get to the region of Moriah. His heart was already heavy from sending his first-born son away, now God is requesting the life of his second son. What's significant about this story is that God was trying to build Abraham's faith in Him. God told Abraham to sacrifice his only son. Though this was a nerve-wracking request, Abraham moved past the doubt, fear, and confusion and focused on the Father. Abraham was prepared to do whatever the Lord commanded him to do. Abraham was tested right up to the point where he

WE CAN'T CONTROL WHAT HAPPENS TO US, BUT WE CAN CONTROL HOW WE RESPOND TO IT.

was about to take his son's life. As Abraham raised his hand with the knife in complete trust and obedience to God, the Lord provided a ram just in time to take the place of his son.

Abraham having real faith in God trusted his trainer. I believe that when the request came to him from God to sacrifice his son he was devastated. One thing that helped Abraham during this time was the acknowledgment that God was the one who gave him his son in the first place. As crazy as sacrificing his son sounded, it sounded just as crazy as him and Sarah having a child at their old age. Abraham had to move past what made sense to him and be obedient to God. It was also important for Abraham not to lose sight of the promises that God gave him. Before those promises were fulfilled, he had to be tested and conditioned to handle what God had in store for him. Some of the trials in our lives come solely to build our faith in God. It's in those times of complete faith and trust in God that we are most connected to Him.

Troubles, hard times, trials, persecution, heartaches, whatever you want to call it will come. What we as Christians must learn to do is never allow the situation to shake our faith. Will you understand it? No. Can you control it? No. We can't control what happens to us, but we can control how we respond to it. This is why it's important that we trust our trainer. God knows exactly what He's doing, and by questioning His actions we're actually questioning our belief in him.

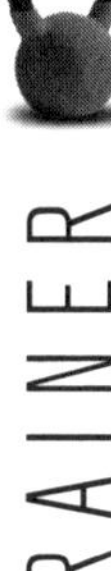

Holly & Seth's Workout Plan

Meet my friends Holly & Seth. Their strength and conditioning workout plan was not only challenging but inspiring as well. Holly and I have been friends since the 8th grade and even graduated from high school together. I met her husband, Seth, in College while he was studying theology. He's now a Pastor in Southern California. Since this chapter is dealing with having faith enough to trust your trainer, I knew their story would be perfect. Holly and Seth are very special people. I don't just say that because they're my friends and I've known them for years, I say that because of their spirits. It's hard to explain, they're just awesome, humble God-fearing people. Once you've spent time in their presence, you can see that the characteristics they possess are of Christ.

Their story begins on a beautiful day in Southern California. Seth was two holes away from completing a round of golf with some friends. As he approached the 16th hole he thought to himself: "There's no better way to spend your day off than to have good fellowship and a good golf game." Immediately after those pleasant thoughts, he got a text message from his pregnant wife. At that point, he noticed he had missed two of her calls. Any husband out there knows that's not a good thing, especially when your wife is pregnant. Seth immediately called Holly and she informed him that while using the restroom she felt a gush of water followed by blood. Since she couldn't reach a doctor, she drove herself to the hospital. When she arrived at the hospital the attending doctor did an examination and realized she was fully dilated and the baby was lying in a breech position. They needed to perform a caesarean section in order for the baby to be born.

As Holly explained the situation to Seth he couldn't help but notice how calm she sounded. It was as if she was not the least bit concerned. Seth on the other hand was frantic and rushed to the hospital. On a ride that seemed like forever, Seth couldn't help but assume the worse. With his emotions running wild he asked himself: Will we lose the baby? Will Holly be okay? Why wasn't I home? His tears flowed as he sped toward the hospital, and all he could say was "JESUS Please!"

As Seth entered the hospital he found the nurses wheeling his new daughter into the NICU. A team of four nurses and one doctor surrounded her as they worked aggressively to stabilize her breathing. As he approached the table the nurses parted and he saw little Emilie Grace. After three hours of intense treatment to stabilize her breathing and heart rate, she was then air-lifted to Kaiser Hospital in Anaheim. As Seth rode with his daughter in the helicopter he had no idea that he had just entered the training gym of faith.

Allow me to give you the whole story. Two months prior to their daughter being born, weighing only 1.4 pounds, Holly and Seth were studying an interesting topic in their morning worship. The topic this young couple was studying was faith. Holly and Seth, both serious about their relationship with God, wanted to have a better understanding of what faith really was. So, being intentional about their quest, they put aside time to study it together. Here's the interesting thing, exactly seven days, one week before Emilie Grace was born, Seth prayed a specific prayer to God. Seth's request to God was to experience real radical faith! Seven days later, his daughter was born.

Can I be honest with you? When I got the news I was distraught. I went to my office, closed the door and cried out to God. I questioned what He was doing, and I asked God Why Holly & Seth? Why would you allow this to happen to them? They're faithful to you. And God spoke to me loud and clear. He said, "It is because of their faithfulness that I allowed this to happen. I can trust them with this experience!" At that time trials made more sense. God was telling me that God He gives us what He knows He can trust us with. He knew that Holly and Seth were spiritually prepared for what was about to take place. So there they were, embarking upon a journey with their personal spiritual trainer that would change their lives forever. Holly and Seth were informed that Emilie had a grade-four brain bleed, the worst their doctors had ever seen. As they sat in the Neonatal waiting room and listened to the doctor give three options the reality of Emilie's condition began to set in. The doctors said option one was to maintain the level of care realizing that their daughter would have severe mental handicaps. Option two was to maintain the same level of care but if her breathing declines, they would not resuscitate her. Option three was to remove all breathing support and they would simply hold their daughter while she slowly died.

It was clear the doctors wanted to use options two or three. From a scientific standpoint a child with a level-four brain bleed has a one in a million chance of recovering. The child's body would grow but the higher-level brain functions and motor skills would remain underdeveloped.

The night before they received this report Seth snuggled into Holly's small hospital bed. They laid there reflecting on the emotional rollercoaster and events from the last few days. The same couple that was studying faith, now wrestled with where their faith would land. Why would God allow this to happen? What did we do wrong? Would we trust God through this storm? These were just a few of the questions they had. Through the questions, they cried, prayed, and held each other close. It was that night that they decided no matter what happened they will trust God for full healing and deliverance!

Like we discovered in this chapter, faith isn't faith until it's tested. Holly and Seth embarked upon a journey of real radical faith. They went to the gym and were getting spiritually fit, but their personal trainer saw fit to have them join the advanced training class. Emilie Grace is doing much better despite what the doctors said. The swelling went down and they now have their daughter home. By no means was it an easy road dealing with multiple test, surgeries, exams, etc. Being in the hospital approximately 150 days is exhausting—physically, mentally and spiritually, but they had to trust their trainer. Emilie is now almost 9 pounds and her beauty is a reflection from God.

It's obvious that some of the crosses we carry are there to simply build our faith and the faith of others. As far as the future of Emilie is concerned, the doctors can say what they want, they don't make life. In fact, they're still "studying" medicine. How dare we as Christians take the doctors' word over God's promises! God does miracles today, and Emilie getting this far and being home now is a miracle. Holly and Seth trust their trainer and still believe the effectual prayers of the righteous avail much. They still believe man doesn't live by bread alone. They still believe every promise of God is yes and amen. They still believe their journey was ordained by God for their good and His glory, and they still believe she is healed!!

Basic Training

1. What physical evidence does Christ have that shows us he's qualified to train us to be spiritually fit?

2. In John 16:33, Jesus tells His disciples that they'll go through hard times, but then He tells them to be of good cheer. Why is that?

3. Will God give you more than you can handle? If so, why?

4. Is faith what we have, or is faith what we practice?

5. Why did God ask Abraham to sacrifice his son?

6. Do you truly trust your trainer "God" with whatever happens in your life?

"Scan the QR Code to view the video for the chapter, or visit our website www.jeremyanderson.org."

Chapter 4

WEIGHT LIFTING

Let's be honest, carrying your cross is a painful process. The cross throughout the Bible symbolizes death, trial and persecution. I remember being in the gym one day working out when I noticed a guy who looked like a professional body builder. I mean, this guy's muscles had muscles. I went over to my fellow body builder [joke] and asked him how he got so muscular. He responded in an angry, aggressive tone; he said 'it took a lot of pain and a whole lot of time.' Seeing that he wasn't in the mood to talk, I went back to my normal workout.

IT'S NOT UNTIL WE'RE WILLING TO SACRIFICE TIME AND COMFORT THAT WE'LL REACH OUR GOALS.

Although his response was short and aggressive, the point was clear. True growth takes time and it can be a painful process. The problem with people today is we want the growth without going through the process. We want the crash diet, easy fix, and get rich quick schemes. The reality is they may work for a short while but the results don't last. It's not until we're willing to sacrifice time and comfort that we'll reach our goals. Setting physical goals are good, but even better than that is growing spiritually.

I Timothy 4:7-8 (NIV): Have nothing to do with godless myths and old wives' tales; rather, train yourself to be godly. For physical training is of some value, but godliness has value for all things, holding promise for both the present life and the life to come.

Here in 1st Timothy, Paul is saying that physical training is good and has a little value but godliness has great value. You see, godliness has value in the present life and the life to come! This body builder in my gym was buff, but was he spiritually fit? I'm sure he went through all sorts of physical pain and was able to endure, but what would happen if he lost his spouse? How would he handle the emotional pains of life? Our physical bodies are great but God's trying to work on our spiritual bodies. If we can take the work ethic of this body builder and apply those principles to our spiritual lives, we would get to another level spiritually.

This body builder was willing to sacrifice his time and comfort to reach his physical goals. He wasn't into fitness Monday-Friday only. Everything about this guy was bodybuilding and fitness. He embraced the pains of the process every day. There was a certain level of consistence he practiced as well.

When he worked out he didn't complain because he knew that in order for his body to get to a certain level there was a certain level of resistance he had to endure. It's the same way in our Christian walk. God, our personal trainer, is not only trying to strengthen our faith in Him, He's also trying to condition us for the kingdom of heaven.

EMBRACE THE STRUGGLE

One thing that a trainer will tell you is that a sure fire way for your muscles to grow is to lift heavy weights. It doesn't really matter the amount of reps you do as long as the weight is heavy enough for you to struggle. True growth takes place when you embrace the struggles of life. Some would say that in the struggle you see what you're made of. I would say, in the struggle you're being made. Everyone wants to be fit, but no one want to go through the pain. Pain is a necessary process of growth.

EVERYONE WANTS TO BE FIT, BUT NO ONE WANT TO GO THROUGH THE PAIN.

Aside from push-ups, the bench-press is one of the more traditional ways to improve your chest muscles. When you're alone and you're working out on the bench it's important that you lift only what you can handle. If you really want to get strong and you're serious about your growth, you'll get someone to spot you. A spotter is someone who stands behind you and assists you with lifting the weight. This is how you exhaust your chest muscles. Here's the reality, when you have someone to spot you, you're able to lift more than you could if you were working out alone. Sound familiar? This is why God at times gives us more than we can bear so we can learn to lean on Him, and from that we'll push more than we would without Him. That's where real growth takes place. This is how you get true strength and growth within your muscles. Here's the reality, the more weight you lift, the stronger you get.

I Chronicles 16:11-12 (NIV): "Look to the Lord and his strength; seek his face always. Remember the wonders he has done, his miracles, and the judgments he pronounced."

Let's be honest, sometimes the weight of the world can get heavy. What happens when the weight of life is just too much for us to lift? You do what any bodybuilder does; you get someone to spot you. Even now as you read this book you might be having a hard time with a situation; this is when it's time to ask God for a spot. The funny thing is that He's been there the whole time making sure that very thing you're trying to lift doesn't crush you. It's only by Jesus spotting us that we're going to get the needed growth anyway. He was the one who allowed the extra weight to be placed on your bar. The great news is that Jesus is saying, "hey, let me help you with that." Where we go wrong as Christians is we try to carry the burdens ourselves.

Matthew 11:28-30 (NIV): "Come to me, all you who are weary and burdened, and I will give you rest. Take my yoke upon you and learn from me, for I am gentle and humble in heart, and you will find rest for your souls. For my yoke is easy and my burden is light."

Here in Matthew Jesus is saying, come to me and find rest, let me lift the weight for you, my yoke is light. You're probably wondering what a yoke is, well it's not the egg yoke so don't get hungry on me. In the Bible when they referenced "yoke" they're speaking of a bar of wood that's constructed to unite two animals (usually oxen) together, thus enabling them to work in the fields bound. This keeps them walking side by side in order to share the load equally. Jesus invites us to take upon ourselves His yoke, which of course is easy. This way He is right beside us carrying the weight. Now we have His constant presence by our side and we can walk together.

GOD EVEN SENT A SPOTTER FOR JESUS WHEN HE WAS CARRYING HIS CROSS.

God even sent a spotter for Jesus when he was carrying his cross. After being beaten, kicked and whipped, Jesus had to carry his own cross to Calvary. I can hardly imagine the pain that was caused by the rugged heavy beam pressing into the bloody shoulders of Jesus. The scourging and loss of blood weakened him so much that he couldn't go on carrying the heavy crossbeam. Apparently at random the soldiers chose Simon of Cyrene and forced him to carry the cross of Christ.

Matthew 27:32 (NIV): "As they were going out, they met a man from Cyrene, named Simon, and they forced him to carry the cross."

You see, Christ knows all too well the pains and struggles of carrying the cross. After getting beaten and tortured nearly to death, Christ started off on his journey carrying his own cross, though the load was too heavy. If Christ got assistance while carrying His cross, how much more will He give you and me assistance? The convicting thing about Christ carrying His cross is that though He was innocent, He never said a mumbling word. I think back on how I complain at the crosses I carry when I'm guilty of sin daily.

God never intended for us to go through our struggles alone. When Philippians says: "I can do all this through Christ who gives me strength," that's real! The key words here are, "through Christ." The reason why the weight tends to crush us is because we don't rely on God to spot us. When we lean on God for His strength and help, that's us practicing common sense and humility. The humility factor comes in because there's a certain level of pride associated with asking for help.

GOD IS INCREASING YOUR FAITH IN HIM THE MORE YOU LIFT.

GETTING STRONGER

Here's the great thing about weight lifting, your strength increases the more you lift. The devil thinks he's slick. Through circumstances, he tries to put extra weight on our bench press thinking we won't be able to lift the bar and we'll be disappointed and leave. With the help of our spotter, we can lift whatever weight is put on the bar. Thus the devil is actually "helping" you get stronger. What Satan meant for bad, God meant for good. So in a spiritual context, God is increasing your faith in Him the more you lift. God knows your spiritual strength and knows exactly how to push you to the next level. Don't take my word for it. Look at the life of Job. Job was so righteous that God actually bragged about him to Satan.

Job 1:8 (NIV): Then the LORD said to Satan, "Have you considered my servant Job? There is no one on earth like him; he is blameless and upright, a man who fears God and shuns evil."

Sounds like bragging to me. Ok, so here's what happened, there's a meeting that Satan invites himself to. Satan felt that the only reason Job was faithful to God was because of all the blessings God gave him. God says ok, lets find out. You can touch all he has except his life. The test for Job's faithfulness began. Tragedy strikes and Job receives word from some of his servants who were spared. One after another they bring news of death and destruction. They tell him that he lost all his cattle, land and, more importantly, the lives of his children. Surely after Satan took all of Job's possessions he would turn from God. Here was Job's response:

Job 1:20-22 (NIV): "At this, Job got up and tore his robe and shaved his head. Then he fell to the ground in worship and said: "Naked I came from my mother's womb, and naked I will depart. The Lord gave and the Lord has taken away; may the name of the Lord be praised." In all this, Job did not sin by charging God with wrongdoing."

That response is crazy right? I don't know about you but after reading this I feel silly about complaining over a lost job or a car accident or relationship problems. Job not only lost his cattle, land, riches but he also lost every single one of his children. Pay close attention to what Job says in verse 21, "the Lord gave and The Lord has taken away, may the name of The Lord be praised."

I guess you could say that Job passed the test God gave him. Once again, God didn't want Job to lose everything, but He allowed it. Think how proud God had to be to trust his servant Job with this type of weight. Remember in chapter 3, we learned that God only gives us what He can trust us with. That's some serious lifting Job had to do. Imagine if you lost your job, your car gets repossessed, your savings account gets depleted and your house is foreclosed all in one day. Then imagine how you'd feel to get a call that same day from your children's middle school only to find that there was a mass shooting and your two children were murdered. While it may seem horrendous and unrealistic that these things could all happen in one day, it closely parallels what happened in Job's life.

SATAN MIGHT DISCOURAGE YOU BUT HE CAN'T DESTROY YOU.

INCREASING THE WEIGHT

At the beginning of chapter 2 in the book of Job we see that Satan went back to God again and God acknowledged that Job (though losing everything) stayed faithful to him. Satan felt that he only stayed faithful because of his health. Satan figured that if Job's health was challenged he would surely turn against God. God saw fit to allow the weight that Job was lifting to be increased. God having faith in his servant Job allowed the enemy to touch his body but would not permit Satan to kill his faithful servant. That's a word for you! Satan might discourage you but he can't destroy you. He might deceive you but he can't delete you. He might even bring doubt but he can't bring defeat!

Once Satan got clearance to further test Job, I can imagine that Satan wasted no time afflicting Job's body. I imagine Job sitting home, still sad at the passing of his children, when his arm begins to itch. As he reaches to scratch his arm, his leg begins to itch. Before long, Job's whole body is in pain. The Bible states that Job had sores and boils from the top of his head to the bottom of his feet. This lasted for months and only got worse. Soon maggots and ulcers covered his body and he had erosion in his bones. Eventually his boils and skin turned black and his bones felts as if they were burning. Can you imagine how painful this felt? Not only was Job's heart broken, his body was broken also. Though Job was faithful to God, his wife's faith wasn't as strong. Heartbroken at the loss of her children and change in social status, Job's wife suggested that Job just curse God and die. Look at Job's response:

Job 2:9-10 (NIV): His wife said to him, "Are you still maintaining your integrity? Curse God and die!" He replied, "You are talking like a foolish woman. Shall we accept good from God, and not trouble?"

Before this great test came, I'm sure Job's wife considered herself "faithful." It's easy to be faithful to God when things were going good. But, oh how things change when our lifestyle, family dynamic or health is challenged. I can understand her pain but what I have a hard time grasping is the faithfulness of Job. This was some heavy weight Job was lifting. Let's look at what happened: God had faith that Job could handle this situation so He allowed it.

Sometimes your faith in God will have to be tested and tried. Just like lifting weights, God saw fit to add more weight to the bar Job was pushing and He was right there to spot him.

NOT ABOUT JOB

I could write a whole book just on the life and story of Job but for now I want to focus on a few points. We know that when Job moved mentally passed his pain and he began to pray for his friends is when he got his breakthrough, and healing took place. We also know that God blessed him and his wife with more land, cattle, and kids than they had before. Job's faithfulness and blessings from God was even passed down to his children. The Bible states how Job's daughters were the finest in the land. That's pretty amazing! God said not only will I give you three daughters but they'll be the finest women around. Now, the Bible never stated Job got a new wife, so this leads us to believe that he stayed with the same woman who suggested he "curse God and die."

Although Job never cursed God, he did question what He was doing and requested to be put to death. During this time God began to ask Job some questions and through most of the book of Job we see how God in His own way showed Job how big and sovereign He was. After this eye-opening experience with God, Job then proclaimed, "I've heard of you but now I've seen you." This experience

THE FAITH OF OTHERS WILL BE INCREASED WHEN GOD BRINGS YOU OUT OF THAT SITUATION.

gave Job a clearer view of the sovereignty of God.

Can you imagine what this did for Job's wife and her faith in God? Because of the faithfulness of her husband, she was blessed. She regained her social status and God blessed her womb to have 10 more children! God knew the heart of Job, but He also knew the heart of his wife. Sometimes God will allow you to go through pain that will ultimately make you stronger. If handled properly, the faith of others will be increased when God brings you out of that situation. Job's situation was of course extreme but it's a word for the world that although God may not cause the pain, He'll allow it to come to increase your faith and to increase the faith of others.

A LESSON FROM JOB

When you look at the story of Job and the conversations he had with his friends it's clear that they thought Job was experiencing those trials because of some great sin he committed. I'm sure after God miraculously healed Job and blessed his land, health and marriage again, their view of God and trials changed. In those days Jews viewed afflictions as some form of penalty for wrongdoing. Unknown to his friends this wasn't the case with Job. Now, it is true that all suffering is the result of transgressing against God's law, "sin." Case in point, if

sin had never come into the world we would not know pain and suffering. Satan, the author of sin and confusion, led men to believe that disease and death came from God as punishment. God needed to give a lesson to mankind to counteract the lies of Satan. The story of Job illustrates that God even allows the righteous to be afflicted by pain and suffering.

Matthew 5:45 (NIV): "He causes his sun to rise on the evil and the good, and sends rain on the righteous and the unrighteous."

No doubt the relationship between Job and God went to another level. God knew Job was faithful but wanted to go deeper with him. What Satan used for evil, God used for Good. We might not be able to understand why we lift the weight we lift but we have to know that God is there to spot us. God knows exactly what you can handle, so when he gives you something you can't handle, ask Him for a spot.

Jaspertena's Workout Plan

Meet my friend Jaspertena; we call her "Jassy" for short. Her strength and conditioning workout plan was both powerful and painful. Jassy dated her high school sweetheart, Darryll for eight years and they got married in 2001. After seven years of marriage, God blessed this family with a handsome and energetic son Darryll, who goes by his middle name, Nathan. She and her husband had great careers, and built a house in Atlanta, Georgia. Things weren't perfect but Jassy had a great life full of blessings.

Jassy was no stranger to pain, she had experienced her share of it and through it all she continually gave God praise. One evening in June 2012, Jassy's life changed forever. It was a normal summer evening with her husband and son. They were finishing up dinner at a restaurant and were headed home. Jassy and her husband had taken separate cars so they agreed that Darryll would take their son, Nathan, home with him. After dinner, Nathan begged his mom to let him ride with her but she had a stop to make after dinner so she sent him home with his father.

After making her stop, Jassy headed home. On the highway near her house she could see large clouds of smoke, which looked like a house fire. Jassy's first thought was, 'I pray that's not my house. Then she thought, 'I pray that's no one's house, and if it is, I pray they're ok.' As she got closer to her subdivision, she knew in fact it was a house fire, and it was on her street. As she pulled into her street, she saw that it was her house on fire and she quickly looked for a place to park. The street was blocked with ambulances, fire trucks and police cars. As Jassy tried to get closer, she wondered where her husband and their four-year-old son were.

The safety officials brought Jassy a chair while they scrambled to get answers. The EMT checked her vitals and saw that she was four and a half months pregnant, so they tried their best to keep her calm. I can only imagine the thoughts that were going through her mind at that time. As she sat waiting, Jassy was reminded of some friends of hers who had lost their child a few weeks prior. While she sat there preparing for the worse, she couldn't help but think of how calm and at peace her friends were considering their tragic loss. With that in mind, Jassy knew she served the same God they did and if God could keep her friends she knew He would keep her.

While Jassy was waiting for her core group of friends to show up, neighbors who served as support surrounded her. Convinced that Satan wouldn't get any victory in this situation, Jassy began to repeat aloud: "God is still God, God is still God." The EMT's looked at her like she was crazy. That's right! In the midst of her house in flames and no sign of her husband and son, she still had the mind to acknowledge God as God. An hour went by and Jassy's close friends began to show up in support. That hour she spent waiting for some answers seemed like forever.

Shortly after her close friends showed up, the Medical Examiner pulled up and Jassy knew then her husband and son were dead. Why else would you need a Medical Examiner but to pronounce them dead? God's timing throughout this whole situation was perfect. He made sure she had her core group of friends around her before she got the tragic news. In the midst of this all the local news stations were like vultures trying to get a statement and pictures of Jaspertena. During this time, in the forefront of her mind she thought: 'No matter what, God's name will be glorified. Was her heart crushed? Yes. Was she in shock? Yes. Did she cry and scream? Of course she did, but she also acknowledged that God was in control.

All at once, Jaspertena lost her home, husband and her son, but what she didn't lose was her faith. In an interview with the local news station she was asked if she ever asked God, "Why me?" Jassy's response was: "No, I asked myself, why not me?" One thing Jassy told me that I find inspiring is that, if God is God on the good days, then God is God on the bad days. If not, then He isn't God. Therefore we should praise and acknowledge Him regardless of the type of day we're having. When the news stations asked for a comment Jassy said that the only thing that came to mind when she addressed them was, "God is still God."

The next few days were rough but God got her through it. Jassy comes from a large family so when her brother and seven sisters, one of them being her twin, came together, their fellowship served as comfort. God used Jassy's local church and friends to support her during that time. People were donating airplane tickets, money, gift cards, etc. They were also cooking food for her, and two couples even donated fully furnished homes for Jassy's family to stay in while visiting. The next step was to plan Darryll's and Nathan's celebration service. That's right, celebration service. Jassy knew her husband didn't want a memorial service; he wanted the family and friends to get together and celebrate their lives, and that's exactly what they did. Their celebration service was like church; lots of singing, testifying and worshiping. Afterwards they even had a social for the people to come and continue to fellowship.

Just like Job had to experience the ridicule from his friends by blaming his condition on some hidden sin, Jassy too had to deal with extra stuff that tried to wear on her spirit. The drama with the insurance companies made the healing process more challenging. Then you have the so-called Christians who would tell her that she was still in shock which is why she was in good spirits. No, she was in good spirits because she was filled with the Spirit of God. The same people who prayed that God give Jassy strength during this time were the same people who questioned where she got her strength from. Makes you wonder if we believe in the things we pray for.

After the celebration service, Jassy's main focus was to take care of the gift that God placed inside of her. Her daughter was due near the end of November. Jassy coming from such a large family didn't want to give birth to her daughter alone, so she had family visit and rotate near the end of her pregnancy. On November 26, 2012 while her family was in town, Jassy gave birth to her beautiful daughter Delaney. As a matter of fact, Delaney came an hour before some of the family members had to leave the hospital to catch flights.

Not only did God bless Jassy with a beautiful daughter to remind her of Darryll and Nathan, He also provided for her needs. Her job gave her paid time off, and after negotiation with the insurance companies, she was able to pay off her house and she still owns the land. In addition to that she has a new beautiful home to raise Delaney in. Just to show you the love of God, everything in the house burned down except her digital camera and a plastic tub of pictures. For a house to burn down and a digital camera and plastic container of pictures survive, is only by the power of God. God knew that Jassy would need those pictures and memories.

Jassy knows that the weight she lifted earlier in life prepared her for this trial. She looks at past pains as training for this situation. Jassy told me that everyone has a testimony, and that there's nothing significant about hers. But I beg to differ. Others may have experienced tragic losses similar to Jassy, but I haven't seen faith like hers. I'm realizing that a testimony isn't about what God delivered us from; the testimony is about how we handled the situation. This is what makes Jassy's story so powerful. She had the mind through it all to proclaim the name of the Lord. Then she went on the news and witnessed to the Atlanta metropolitan area that has over 5.4 million people. God was able to trust Jassy with this type of platform. Just think of the 5.4 million people who live in the Atlanta metropolitan area and the impact her story made on their lives. This is the impact a true modern disciple makes. From this weight lifting experience, Jassy is even stronger than before and still proclaiming the name of the Lord.

Basic Training

1. In 1st Timothy 4, what does Paul say is better than physical training?

____

____

2. What's the importance of having someone spot you while working out?

____

____

3. Who is your spiritual spotter?

____

____

4. Why did God allow Satan to afflict Job?

____

____

5. What was Job's response to losing his possessions and children?

____

____

6. At what point did Job experience his breakthrough and healing?

____

____

WEIGHT LIFTING

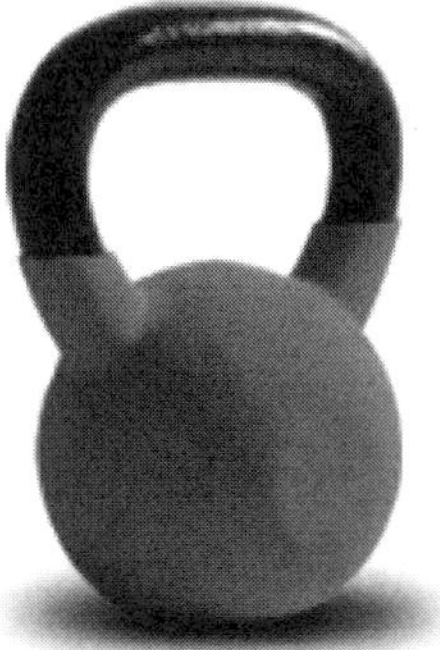

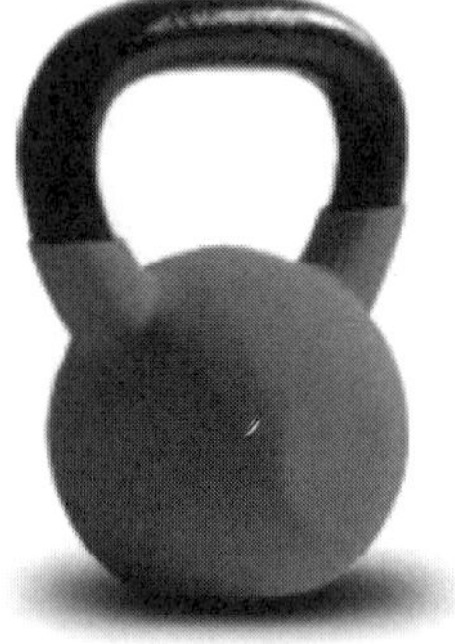

"Scan the QR Code to view the video for the chapter, or visit our website www.jeremyanderson.org."

Chapter 5

CARDIO

Can I be honest with you? I've been working out for years, but one area I've always dreaded was cardio. I can honestly say that I despise running. God challenged me at the beginning of 2013 to embrace the areas in my life where I was weakest. I was one of those people who was in shape but wasn't in shape. What I mean is I was consistently working on the areas of my body that people could see. I would work on my biceps, triceps, chest, back, and abdominal area. I would even work my legs a bit, but cardio - No Way!

Cardio is one of those areas that you work on but you don't always see the results you want. I always felt that God gave us the ability to run fast just in case a lion or dog was chasing us. Besides that, why would someone need to run fast or for long distance? I know now that in order for us to be strengthened and conditioned cardio is imperative.

Your heart is the most important muscle you have!

The best way to give this muscle a workout is to get it beating faster and keep it there for an extended period of time. By doing this your body will be much more efficient at transporting the blood and nutrients throughout the body that it needs. It will also increase the amount of oxygen the body can use at any given point in time, and it keeps your blood pressure and heart rate in check.

A HEART LIKE JESUS

I've learned that some of the trials we as Christians experience give us a deeper sense of what others are going through. It's really hard as Christians to feel empathetic for someone if we don't know what they've gone through. Having a heart like Jesus is a heart that's caring and empathetic. Unfortunately, it's not until we experience our own traumatic event that we're able to relate to someone less fortunate. It's not that we don't care, it's just that sometimes we're busy and disconnected. The world today moves so fast that when we hear about someone's problem or pain we lift them in prayer and then move on with our lives; their pain rarely pierces our hearts. A truly caring spirit is lacking in the hearts of Christians today.

Ezekiel 36:26 (NIV): "I will give you a new heart and put a new spirit in you; I will remove from you your heart of stone and give you a heart of flesh."

This passage comes from Ezekiel when God was assuring Israel of their restoration. Just like the children of Israel, God is trying to restore the lives of His children but first He has to give us a new and clean heart. Without Him we don't know how to be compassionate toward others. Once God replaces our heart of stone with a heart of flesh he can truly use us.

{ COMPASSION IS A CHARACTER TRAIT OF JESUS HIMSELF. }

In chapter one we discussed how members of God's church are all in one body. If we are truly in the body of Christ when one of our members hurt, we should all hurt because we are part of one body. God, at times, will allow you to carry a cross so that you can know how others feel. When we're able to relate to the pains of others, we begin to birth a sense of compassion within our heart. Compassion is a character trait of Jesus himself. This is why the Bible states that we don't have a God who looks low and doesn't understand our pain. We can approach our God of grace with confidence that we'll receive mercy because He understands the pains we endure!

Hebrews 4:15-16 (NIV): "For we do not have a high priest who is unable to empathize with our weaknesses, but we have one who has been tempted in every way, just as we are—yet he did not sin. Let us then approach God's throne of grace with

confidence, so that we may receive mercy and find grace to help us in our time of need."

STAMINA

Did you know that when you have a cardio workout while running you're actually building up your stamina? The same is in our spiritual experience. God is building up our stamina through the trials we endure. The more we endure, the more we run and the longer we can go. Many of us have constant pains and struggles that we deal with. The very crosses we carry condition our hearts for others who are carrying similar crosses. These situations also make us more mature and able to embrace the pains of life. In addition to all of this, it's the spiritual stamina that we gain from the pain. I know there are times when you're simply tired of carrying your cross, but I find encouragement from Isaiah when he states that if our hope is in God, He'll renew our strength and we won't get weary!

Isaiah 40:31 (NIV): "but those who hope in the Lord will renew their strength. They will soar on wings like eagles; they will run and not grow weary ,they will walk and not be faint."

Now we know that the race isn't given to the strong or the swift. The race is given to the one who hangs in there until the end. Through our trials God is trying to strengthen us to be able to endure to the end. Spiritual cardio also builds up a spiritual stamina, which is used in our Christian walk. It may be rough, it may be hard, but just keep on pushing. Paul discusses this in the book of Hebrews.

Hebrews 12:1-3 (NIV): "Therefore, since we are surrounded by such a great cloud of witnesses, let us throw off everything that hinders and the sin that so easily entangles. And let us run with perseverance the race marked out for us, fixing our eyes on Jesus, the pioneer and perfecter of faith. For the joy set before him he endured the cross, scorning its shame, and sat down at the right hand of the throne of God. Consider him who endured such opposition from sinners, so that you will not grow weary and lose heart."

A BROKEN & CONTRITE HEART

God wants to break your heart. Salvation is possible due to the deep love and compassion that God has for us. The problem is that our view of sin is distorted. We view sin as a little decision we make that's not "*that bad.*" When we lose a loved one, or go to a third world country and see real poverty, it should not only move us to action but should scream to us, "*hey I'm the effects of sin!*" The reason for this is that pain and sufferings in the world are all the effects of sin. It's in those times of pain and suffering

{ GOD WANTS TO BREAK YOUR HEART. }

that sin doesn't seem so simple. The pains of life should move us to repentance. When I deal with a trial and my experiences push me to my mental limit, I instantly get angry at Satan. It's the weirdest thing, but when I or my family gets attacked it fuels me to minister even more. My advice to you is to view the pains in life as the effects of sin and you'll begin to view sin differently.

The whole idea of this book is to help you understand that the trials we experience and the crosses we carry are there to strengthen our faith and condition us for the kingdom of heaven. When your heart is broken and contrite, the sincerity of your character is closest to God. The constant pains in your life are there so that you can have a broken heart and a contrite spirit. When we get to this point we're willing to do anything and everything for God, and we have a true hatred for sin. David even said that the Lord is near to those with a broken heart.

Psalms 34:18 (NKJV): "The Lord is near to those who have a broken heart, and saves such as have a contrite spirit.

Psalms 51:17 (NIV): My sacrifice, O God, is a broken spirit; a broken and contrite heart you, God, will not despise.

God wants us to get to a point that the effects of sin actually move us to true repentance. He wants us to be honest, sincere and open with how we feel. We see here in Psalms 34, that He is drawn close to those with a broken heart. God can understand and feel your emotions and pain. Unfortunately, it takes major heartache for the effects of sin to hit home; for true remorse to take place.

THE LOVE LETTER

The relationship between Paul and Timothy was quite encouraging. In 1st Timothy 1:2, Paul referenced Timothy as his *"true child in faith."* When it came to Timothy, Paul had a conditioned heart, which is why he wrote the letters of encouragement to him. You see Paul's heart was conditioned from countless beatings and imprisonment that came from spreading the gospel of Jesus Christ. He knew how it felt to be on the front line while enduring the cross, which is what compelled him to write the letter of encouragement to Timothy. You see, if Paul had not endured what he did he might not have understood the importance of encouragement. Sometimes people just need to know that you've been where they are and that they're going to be okay.

II Timothy 4:5 "But you, keep your head in all situations, endure hardship, do the work of an evangelist, discharge all the duties of your ministry."

Here in II Timothy, Paul is telling Timothy to endure hardships and to continue to do the work of an evangelist. Paul knew how it felt to endure hardships, imprisonment and pain. As a matter of fact, Paul wrote this letter from prison while awaiting his execution. This, my friends, is the life of a true disciple. I am always impressed by the discipline of Paul. Here Paul is about to be put to death and he uses his last bit of time and energy to encourage Timothy.

Paul's Cardio workout worked well. This is what love looks like and this can only be done with a conditioned and healthy heart. You never see Paul complaining in the letters he wrote to Timothy. You only see one disciple encouraging another. Because of the testimony, love and strength of Paul, Timothy was able to finish his work.

WHAT YOU'RE GOING THROUGH MIGHT NOT EVEN BE ABOUT YOU.

The whole idea of this chapter is for you to wrap your mind around the thought that what you're going through might not even be about you. I know that at the time the pain of what you're experiencing feels like it's about you but that doesn't mean it is. A healthy Christian/disciple should look to the testimony in the midst of it all.

Your pain, once conquered, can be someone else's gain. That's what happens when you share your testimony. When you experience hard times and you make it through you've got to share it. The pain you overcame can be a testimony once you share it. Until then, it's only an experience. It's when you share the deliverance of God that it becomes a testimony because you're testifying to the grace, mercy and power of God. Your testimony is essential to the growth and deliverance of others.

Revelations 12:11 (KJV): "And they overcame him by the blood of the Lamb, and by the word of their testimony"

This is why Jesus said what He said in John 16:33. He told His disciples that they would go through rough times, but just how He overcame they would also. There is victory in your testimony! Do you feel like you're going through a long drawn out trial? Do you feel like you're running a race that will never end? This is God's cardio workout for your life. Allow God to condition your heart and find your testimony at the end of the race.

Ryan & Charisse's Workout Plan

Meet my friends Ryan & Charisse. Their strength and conditioning workout plan was unfortunate yet encouraging. This beautiful and amazing couple got married in 2009, just a few months before my wife and I were married. In November of 2010 Charisse got great news—she was expecting a baby! My wife and I were extremely excited for them! Our joy increased when we found out they wanted us to be the godparents. We were honored. In March of 2011, they found out that the baby was going to be a boy and his name would be Ryan, after his father. Like most couples, they began to plan for their baby boy's entry into the world. The Felton's spent the next few months making preparations for baby Ryan's arrival. Charisse, loving to decorate, went all out with the decorations for little Ryan's room. His room had a jungle theme full of animals and colors.

One morning, Charisse felt a dull ache in her back and found it extremely hard to sleep. During this time Ryan was out of town on business so Charisse asked her mother to take her to the hospital. Charisse was already scheduled for a doctor's appointment that morning so they waited until 7:35am, which was her scheduled time to see what was causing the pain. At the doctor's office, Charisse and her mother went to the back so the nurses could do their regular check on Charisse and the baby's heart rate. After a few times of checking with no results, they figured he was playing hard to get. After a few more times, the nurses decided to perform an ultrasound. By this time, Charisse knew something was going on but wasn't thinking the worst.

As the ultrasound was being performed, Charisse caught a glimpse of the screen and her doctor's face. Then, in an instant, the worst happened. Her doctor said, "Charisse, there is no heartbeat in this baby." Upon hearing that, Charisse cried out, "Nooooo!" This had to be a dream, she had to be mistaken, she thought! How could this happen? What did I do to deserve this? What am I going to tell my husband? These were all questions Charisse asked herself in that little moment that seemed like eternity. While fighting through the tears the doctor dropped another bombshell on Charisse and informed her that since baby Ryan was considered full term, she had to deliver him.

Imagine the mental anguish and pain Charisse was feeling. She had gone in for her routine check-up expecting to hear Ryan's heart beat and maybe deliver early, only to be told her baby died. And to top it off, the doctors needed Charisse to deliver this baby. They even told Charisse to think about burial options! Charisse immediately called her husband Ryan and broke the news to him. This of course broke him down as well. For Ryan being miles away from home made this whole situation worse. Ryan rushed back in town to be by his wife's side. Seeing the pain she endured crushed his heart to the core. Ryan then began to blame himself for everything that was happening. I'll never forget the day I got the call telling me what happened. I was on my way to Illinois to do a taping for a show and had to pull over to the side of the road. I couldn't believe what I was hearing. My first thought was, 'what was God doing?'

Preparations were made and, with her husband by her side, Charisse delivered their precious son. How can a parent prepare for such a thing? The Lord surrounded them with lots of love from family, friends and pastors. This next year would be rough for the Felton's. Through the healing process of losing her son, Charisse was extremely angry. She was angry with God for taking her precious baby away and still allowing abusers, murderers, molesters, and child neglectors to have their babies. She was angry with every mother and their new baby. Charisse struggled with the question of why this had to happen to her and not others. Ryan struggled with the pain of losing his son as well. Ryan really struggled with the grieving process because he was fighting to be strong for his family. He felt that this happened because of the wrong decisions he made in his life.

Charisse was going through a pruning process and was soon able to rejoice through her sorrows. During this time she had three miscarriages. Through the power of God, Charisse became intentional about her healing and began to share her testimony with others. She even began to write. It started with a sentence, then a sentence turned into a paragraph. Eventually the paragraphs turned into pages, and the pages into chapters, then into a whole book. She met and spoke to women who lost their babies and they ministered to one another, which became healing to them all.

After healing took place, Ryan and Charisse went to a Christian specialist to explore the options and possibilities of them having another child. He ran tests that provided answers and they began the physical healing process. He assured them that they were going to have a baby. Fast forward months later, they found out that they were having another beautiful baby boy! They decided to name him Christian Ryan Felton. Such a fitting name for a young man! During the third trimester they experienced lots of scary complications but God kept the baby. December came and in her 34th week of pregnancy, baby Christian was born into the world. Due to complications, baby Christian was in NICU for two weeks before they released him. The doctors spoke of several complications that Christian would face due to genetics and him being a preemie. Christian weighed four pounds fourteen ounces when he was born, and now he's nine months and weighs eighteen pounds three ounces.

Here's the interesting thing about their story: When baby Christian was born and spent those two weeks in the NICU, there was a baby named Zander in the incubator next to Christian. Zander and Christian were actually born on the same day. Ryan being outgoing began to build relationships with Zander's parents. Unfortunately, after two weeks of being in the NICU, Zander died. The feelings that Zander's parents had were all too familiar to Ryan and Charisse. At this time their relationship with God was null so the weight of losing a child crushed them even more.

Before Zander died, Ryan was able to build a relationship, encourage and pray with his mother and father. Since Ryan's heart was conditioned He could empathize with the couple. Tyler (Zander's father) told his whole family about his friendship and relationship with Ryan and Charisse. Because of the power of the Holy Spirit working through Ryan and Charisse, Tyler got his family back in church and reconnected to Jesus! After Ryan's and Charisse's *spiritual cardio* workout, God conditioned their hearts for ministry. Charisse wrote a book titled *"Through the eyes of a grieving Mother,"* and God used Ryan to minister to the Zander family, which ultimately lead them back to Christ.

What's amazing about the Felton's story is that they were able to grow through their pain, and for others it became gain. Some of the storms we endure are to bring us to an intimate place with God, while conditioning our hearts to reach others who may have experienced similar trials. Just like Paul was able to write to Timothy to encourage him, Charisse was able to write her book to encourage other women, and Ryan was able to re-introduce a family to Christ.

Basic Training

1. What does Paul say in Hebrews about God understanding our pain?

2. Why is it so important to have a heart like Jesus?

3. What does Isaiah say about stamina?

4. Why did Paul write that letter to Timothy?

5. What does Psalms say about a broken heart and contrite spirit?

6. What training are you learning from your present trial?

7. Who has God placed in your life for you to help spiritually train?

8. How can you begin to implement these training techniques into your everyday activity or life?

"Scan the QR Code to view the video for the chapter, or visit our website www.jeremyanderson.org."

Chapter 6

BURNING FAT

Let's be honest here, most people join the gym to lose weight, get toned, to live a healthier lifestyle or all the above. Either way you can't lose weight and get toned without first burning fat away. Where does fat come from? From personal experience I would say sweets are the main reason people have excess fat in their bodies. Sugar is the number #1 cause of fat build-up in the body. It's sad that something that tastes so good can be so bad for you. Here's a reality, fat builds up due to our calorie intake, so when we consume more calories than we burn off, it turns to fat.

The key to burning fat is having the right diet. You also need to stay active so you can burn excess calories. Jillian Michaels from the TV show "The Biggest Loser", states in her latest DVD that boosting your metabolism is a great way to help you burn fat. The more intense your workout, the more calories you'll burn. You not only burn more calories while you're working out, but also you're helping your metabolism stay in a higher gear hours after your workout. I

> **SOMETIMES THE PAIN AND TRIALS WE ENDURE COME FROM OUR DISOBEDIENCE.**

know people who workout just to be able to eat what they want. That's a whole different chapter in itself.

In order for us to burn fat, we have to do some extreme exercise to help burn the calories we intake. In this chapter, I'll be referring to the fat build-up as the sin in our lives. God, being our personal trainer provides workouts in our lives so that we can burn the sin from our lives. One would say that the intensity of your workout is based upon what you put into your body. The level of your workout is dependent upon the amount of calories that need to be burned. This means the sinner who's openly sinning and living outside of God's will has to experience a different type of conditioning so that they can become fit for the kingdom. Sometimes the pain and trials we endure come from our disobedience.

BLAMING GOD

It's interesting how we can openly sin, choose our will over God's will, and then blame Him for the consequences of our actions. I'll never forget the time I got a call from a friend of mine who was crying uncontrollably. She had just found out she was expecting a baby, and the father was a man twice her age. I tried to calm her down and asked her to explain the situation to me. After she calmed down, she informed me that she was having twins.

This young lady in her twenties already had a 5-year-old child and now she was expecting twins by a man she had no future plans with. As she sobbed, she made a statement so ridiculous it almost made me laugh. She said, "Why would God do this to me." I was speechless. I didn't know how to handle that statement. Was she really blaming God for *her* actions?

Did God tell her to sleep with this man? Did God tell her to have unprotected sex? Hey, we all make mistakes but to blame our actions on God, that's silly. Realizing the fragile condition she was in, I carefully shared with her how unfair it was to blame God for our choices. This situation is similar to a person who eats cakes, cookies and brownies all day, then blames their personal trainer because they're not seeing the results they want. Here's a harsh reality, some of us construct the very crosses we carry. What I'm saying here is that if we live outside of God's will there's a price to pay. Just as the personal trainer has to help their trainee burn off excess fat that they've added due to an unhealthy diet, God has to help us burn off the extra fat from the sin that plagues our souls.

Ephesians 5:15-17 (NIV): "Be very careful, then, how you live—not as unwise but as wise, making the most of every opportunity, because the days are evil. Therefore do not be foolish, but understand what the Lord's will is."

GOD IS VESTED IN THE GROWTH OF OUR SPIRITUAL LIVES.

We're warned here in Ephesians to be cautious of what we do and how we live. How often do we blame God for what we've done? Often times, as Christians, we'll blame God for our spiritual obesity. When I speak of spiritual obesity I'm speaking of the excessive sins in our lives that weigh us down. There's a certain lifestyle that God is calling us to live. When we don't live that lifestyle then we have to be prepared to make the necessary adjustments. God only wants the best for us so being our personal trainer, He has to guide us to work off that fat we put on. Like we discussed in the first few chapters, God is vested in the growth of our spiritual lives.

High blood pressure, diabetes, cancer, and heart disease can all be attributed to a poor diet. I know this sounds harsh but the truth is when you're experiencing these types of medical issues, you typically have no one to blame but yourself. The same applies to some of the trials we endure. They are the direct effect of the lifestyle we're living. Throughout this book we've discussed how some of the crosses we carry God allows for our spiritual growth, but there are some crosses we carry that we made ourselves.

FAT & COMPLACENT

Spiritual obesity in our lives does not necessarily come from living a life of sin. Our excessive build-up can also come from living a life of complacency. In these last days God is building up an army of bold soldiers for Himself and there's no room for complacency. The problem is that we, as Christians, are too comfortable. We don't mind serving God as long as His requirements don't interfere with our plans. As long as our level of service is contingent upon our level of comfort, God can't effectively use us. In order to get us fit for service, God will send us a fat burning workout that may be painful at times but will ultimately get us spiritually fit.

All fat isn't visible. Some of the fat in our body cannot be seen with the physical eye. People from the outside can't even tell that we're out of shape. The good thing is that our personal trainer, Jesus, knows every detail about our spiritual body. Just as the out-of-shape person is weak, so can we be weak in the service of our Lord. Here's an honest point: The devil isn't impressed that you go to church, nor is he impressed with your John 3:16 bumper sticker. As long as you're comfortable and not spreading the gospel he doesn't care. So what you give a faithful tithe and offering. What if God told you to give double or better yet, quit your job to start a ministry? How will you handle the request from God when it causes you to leave your comfort zone?

JONAH'S DISOBEDIENCE

I'm convinced that our disobedience to God results in us being spiritually fat. God, as our personal trainer, helps us burn the spiritual fat. Being spiritually obese doesn't necessarily mean that you're living a wild and sinful lifestyle. It could simply mean that you're not following the will of God. Jonah, a prophet of God, knows all too well about living outside of God's will and having to deal with the consequences.

Looking at the life of Jonah, he was used by God and he was also a prophet of God. But like many of us, Jonah was out of shape. To outsiders, Jonah looked spiritually fit. He was a known servant for God but God saw the spiritual fat build up deep within his soul. It was evident that Jonah was out of shape when God requested that Jonah go to Nineveh to preach a word of warning. But out of fear for his life, Jonah ran. Jonah was operating in a mode of complacency, which was unacceptable to God. Jonah was comfortable and complacent therefore when God challenged him to step out of his comfort zone he broke his covenant with God and fled to Tarshish.

In view of Jonah's open rebellion, God sent a violent storm. We all know about the storms that God can send. I had rebellious days earlier in my life, and God would send a storm to get me right back on track! God's storms have a way of breaking us, and

> **GOD'S STORMS HAVE A WAY OF BREAKING US.**

that's exactly what happened. The storm that God sent threatened to break the ship to pieces. The crew was terrified and eventually determined that Jonah was responsible for the storm. Jonah acknowledged that he was the cause of the storm and told them to throw him overboard. They initially tried rowing to shore but the waves were too high. Having experienced the power of God, the sailors tossed Jonah into the sea, and the water immediately grew calm.

Once Jonah hit the water, God sent a whale to swallow him up. Jonah had three days to sit in the belly of the whale reflecting on his disobedience to God. I can only imagine what it was like in the belly of that enormous fish. Dead fish, molded seaweed, water, etc. I imagine Jonah floating trying to stay above the water gasping for air in the belly of that whale. The smell had to be absolutely horrendous! Here's the interesting thing, God never intended for Jonah to be in the whale. This was a result of Jonah's decisions. In all actuality, Jonah placed himself in the belly of the whale by being disobedient to God. After three days God commanded the whale to vomit His stubborn prophet onto dry land.

Jonah 2:9-10 (NIV): "But I, with shouts of grateful praise, will sacrifice to you. What I have vowed I

will make good. I will say, 'Salvation comes from the Lord. And the Lord commanded the fish, and it vomited Jonah onto dry land."

Don't miss the significance of what Jonah 2:9-10 says. The Lord commanded the fish and it vomited Jonah onto dry land. You see while Jonah was in the deep sea in the belly of the whale, he was crying out and praying to God. His prayers soon turned to praises in the belly of the whale. The Bible doesn't state that the whale vomited Jonah into the sea; it says that he was delivered to dry land. You see, while Jonah was praising, his praises to God moved the large fish to the shore. Jonah's deliverance was in his repentance and praises to God.

Jonah now on dry land gave his full attention to God. I can imagine Jonah kissing the ground he was on, glad that God had spared his life. Embracing the seriousness of God's mission, Jonah obeyed God and went to Nineveh. When he arrived in Nineveh, he proclaimed that in forty days the city would be destroyed. To Jonah's surprise, the Ninevites believed the message and repented, wearing sackcloth and covering themselves in ashes. Because of their repentance, God had compassion on them and did not destroy them.

SALVATION IN THE WHALE

God is sovereign. Had God not sent that whale, Jonah would have died at sea. Had the sailors not

> **THE THING THAT ALMOST CONSUMED JONAH WAS THE VERY THING THAT SAVED HIS LIFE.**

cast Jonah into the sea, they all might have perished in the storm. Jonah's disobedience could have cost many lives. Just as God sent Jonah to warn Nineveh to repent and be saved, God sent the whale to Jonah for him to repent. God could have destroyed Jonah for his disobedience but instead the grace of God stepped in. The thing that almost consumed Jonah was the very thing that saved his life. I can imagine Jonah complaining in the belly of the whale and then commonsense kicked in. He viewed the whale as a blessing from God, which is what changed his complaining to worship. The whale swallowing Jonah up was actually a sign of God's love for him.

Hebrews 12:5-6 (NIV): "And have you completely forgotten this word of encouragement that addresses you as a father addresses his son? It says, "My son, do not make light of the Lord's discipline, and do not lose heart when he rebukes you, because the Lord disciplines the one he loves, and he chastens everyone he accepts as his son"

Here in Hebrews we see that God disciplines His children out of love. How often do we find ourselves in the belly of a whale? Some of us are going through specific trials that God never intended for us to endure but because of the decisions we made we find ourselves in the belly of the whale. Here's an interesting idea, view the situation you're in as a workout. God will allow the trials to come to burn the sin from your life. You see God is trying to get us spiritually fit but some of us aren't living right, so God brings salvation in the form of a whale. Do you feel swallowed up or consumed by your situation? It will get better. Salvation can be found in the very situation you're going through.

Hebrews 12:7-9 (NIV): "Endure hardship as discipline; God is treating you as his children. For what children are not disciplined by their father? If you are not disciplined—and everyone undergoes discipline—then you are not legitimate, not true sons and daughters at all. Moreover, we have all had human fathers who disciplined us and we respected them for it. How much more should we submit to the Father of spirits and live!"

Here in Hebrews, Paul is saying that you're truly God's children if He trains or disciplines you. He also states that we have human fathers and we respect them so we should also respect God for loving us enough to discipline us. Enduring hardships is exactly what Jonah had to do. The workout that Jonah went through was used to burn the fat from His life. God wanted to execute his will through Jonah but He had to first get him spiritually fit.

Hebrews 12:10-11 (NIV): "They disciplined us for a

little while as they thought best; but God disciplines us for our good, in order that we may share in his holiness. No discipline seems pleasant at the time, but painful. Later on, however, it produces a harvest of righteousness and peace for those who have been trained by it."

TO BECOME INHABITANTS OF OUR INHERITANCE, GOD NEEDS TO BURN THE SINS OUT OF OUR LIVES!

So what Paul is saying here in verse ten is that God wants us to be holy, and that God disciplines us for our own good. Let's be clear here, God doesn't like to see us go through pain but He also knows that in order for you and me to become inhabitants of our inheritance, God needs to burn the sins out of our lives!

There was something within Jonah that made him flee God. Jonah had seen the power of God before. Something was happening within Jonah for him to be able to hear the command of God and still refuse to follow through. God knew that in order for Jonah to remain his prophet, Jonah's sin and complacency needed to be burned away. There was a new level that God wanted to bring Jonah to but first He had to burn away the fat. Look at your life. What is God asking you to do? What's the Nineveh that you're running from? Maybe you've found yourself in the belly of the whale.

Psalms 51:10 (NIV): "Create in me a pure heart, O God, and renew a steadfast spirit within me."

God knew that Jonah needed a clean and pure heart in order to use him on that next level. Not only did Jonah not want to preach for fear of losing his life, he didn't think the people of Nineveh were worthy of the grace of God. The cross Jonah carried was needed so that he could burn the fat from his spiritual body.

Jason's Workout Plan

Meet my friend Jason. His fat burning workout plan was painful and purposeful. He has a story that I feel is perfect for this chapter, for he too knows where a total commitment to God can land him. I've known Jason for about four years and he's always been a cool guy. When it comes to music, he has a unique gift, which he uses by playing the organ at my church. Although Jason had unique gifts and talents, Jason was comfortable. He knew he wasn't living his life in total surrender to God.

On May 31, 2011, Jason was driving from Toronto, Canada back to Huntsville, Alabama; it was a 14-hour trip that Jason was used to making. Jason is originally from Toronto so this was a trip he made all throughout college. At a minimum, Jason had taken this trip and route at least 12 times. This trip however would be the one that changed his life forever. You see Jason lived his life serving God but he knew deep down inside God was asking him for more. In a way Jason was lukewarm. He knew there was hidden potential inside of him but wasn't fulfilling his true purpose.

In route to Huntsville, Jason was cruising through the city of Sarnia, 45 minutes from the U.S. boarder. While driving his black, 2001 Volvo S60, he listened to the audiobook The Shack. During the drive, Jason was questioning God and really wondered if He was real. This doubt in God was in spite of the many times God showed himself to Jason. As he pondered and questioned, a deer walked out onto the highway right in front of Jason's car! Attempting to miss the deer, Jason crashed and was thrown through the front windshield of his Volvo and landed on the road. Not only was Jason thrown from the car, but he landed on the opposite side of the highway!

Not knowing what had just happened Jason woke up for a brief moment in the ambulance as the paramedics took him to London General Hospital for emergency treatment. Jason woke up the next day with multiple bones shattered in his face, missing teeth, cuts through his lips, two fractured ribs, a punctured lung and glass in his skin. I recall seeing the pictures online of his face and I literally couldn't tell it was him, due to the severe swelling in his face.

Jason awoke in the hospital and realized the severity of what had happened. Regardless of the situation, gratitude filled his heart. Jason stayed in the hospital for three days and then they released him. As healing was taking place in his body, spiritual healing was taking place in his heart. Recognizing how God spared his life, Jason felt in a personal way the sovereignty and power of God. Considering how God spared his life, it was at that time that Jason would repay God by going to Nineveh.

Jason's Nineveh was him living his life on purpose. Jason's new purpose wasn't just music because he was already talented. Jason's purpose was to bring glory to God in every area of his life.

Jason had a near-death experience just like Jonah. Jason was called to minister just like Jonah. Jason questioned God just like Jonah. And just like Jonah, Jason failed to submit completely to God. Just like Jonah had a whale, Jason also had a whale, which was his Volvo S60. Jonah found salvation when he was spit out of the mouth of the whale and Jason found deliverance when he was spit out of the windshield of his car. He, like Jonah, was running from his true purpose in life. Painful event, yes, but was it worth it? Yes! His redemption was when he was spit out of the windshield of his car. Though salvation was in their whales, the true deliverance took place when Jason and Jonah were thrown from the very things that were carrying them.

What makes Jason's story even more powerful is the way in which he started his ministry. After the accident, Jason went public with his experiences and shared how God delivered him. In addition to him being vocal about his deliverance, he also began to write. He kept a daily journal of the painful healing process. In the midst of his pain and suffering he saw fit to worship and proclaim the power of God. It was in those moments that he found the needed strength to press on. While vocal with his spiritual and physical healing, Jason saw the difference he was making and realized that he wasn't only talented in the area of music but God had given him a distinct gift to write. I remember reading some of his post on Facebook thinking he was quoting Max Lucado. When I realized it was his writings, I was astonished. We then began to talk about him sharing his story through a book.

At that point in his life, Jason was running to his Nineveh. Jason knew that God had a purpose for him so he used everything within his power to pursue his purpose. Jason wasted no time with his newfound gift and purpose. Jason is now the published author of his book, *25 & Counting*. He travels and preaches, helping people to, "Live their life on Purpose." In addition to all of this, Jason also wrote and recorded an EP Album entitled "Love Letters." Everything that Jason does now is to glorify God.

The workout plan that God put Jason on was one that not only woke him up spiritually but it resuscitated his soul and activated his purpose. Jonah lost his way because he was living his life fulfilling his will as opposed to the will of God. So God sent a whale to get His attention. Sometimes God will have us carry a cross that will eventually bring us closer to him, and activate his will in our lives.

Basic Training

1. What fat "sins" in your life does God want to burn away so you can be fit for Him?

 ____
 ____

2. What was the main reason Jonah wanted to avoid going to Nineveh?

 ____
 ____

3. What fears do you have that's stopping you from fulfilling your purpose in life?

 ____
 ____

4. What did God use to save Jonah's life?

 ____
 ____

5. What reason did Hebrews chapter 12 give for God disciplining His children?

 ____
 ____

6. How do Jonah's and Jason's attitude compare with your attitude during your training? What can you focus on to help with your attitude? Jonah 2:9-10 & Hebrews 12:7

 ____
 ____

7. What life predicament, restriction and/or trial is God using to trim or burn the fat off you?

 ____
 ____

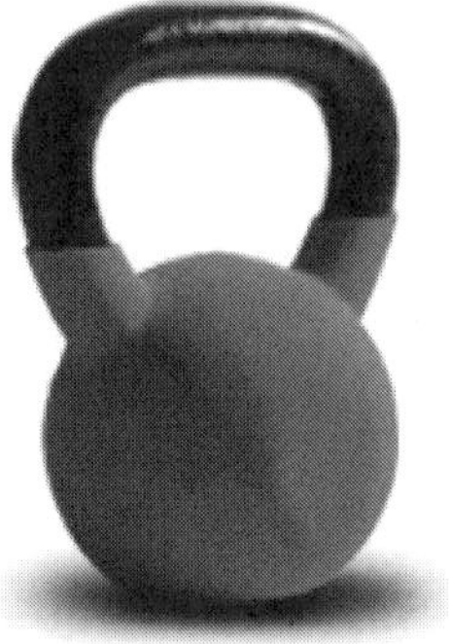

"Scan the QR Code to view the video for the chapter, or visit our website www.jeremyanderson.org."

Chapter 7

DIET

Throughout this whole book we've been discussing ways to become spiritually fit through the crosses we carry. In this final chapter we'll discuss the importance of having a healthy spiritual diet, which is essential to your spiritual growth and development. The reason some people aren't physically fit and have difficulty meeting their physical goal is due to a poor diet. You can buy all the necessary workout attire—shorts, tee shirts, sneakers and headbands, and still be out of shape. You can exercise consistently and only see limited physical results because of a poor diet. Why? The simple fact is you can't put junk in your body and expect to get fit. The problem isn't your efforts in the gym; the problem is your diet outside the gym.

Ask any real Nutritionist or Fitness Trainer, and they'll tell you that in order for you to reach your physical and health goals there are two things you must focus on: diet & exercise. Why is diet so important? Our diet is what conditions us for the trial.

ARE YOU PREPARED TO OPERATE AT THE HIGHEST LEVEL SPIRITUALLY?

The same way it's suggested that your diet has a direct effect on your physical growth, is the same in the spiritual. The crosses we carry and the trials we endure are spiritual training, and what our minds consume have a direct impact on our spiritual development.

Chip Kelly, former head coach of the University of Oregon, left college football and transitioned to the NFL. Upon signing a contract to be the head coach of the Philadelphia Eagles, he made diet and nutrition a priority. Coach Kelly knew the importance of having a well-tuned machine, so he had the team on a special diet to make sure they were prepared to operate at an optimal level. Are you prepared to operate at the highest level spiritually? What you put in your body determines the level of success you achieve.

CONDITIONING OF THE MIND

What you feed your body has a direct effect on how your body performs. The same is true for your mind. What we feed our brains has a direct effect on how we connect with God. Last time I checked, it wasn't your feet, back or chest that connected you to God. It's your brain. The battle for our salvation is taking place in our minds. The question is are you fighting on enemy territory? How can one claim

WHAT WE FEED OUR BRAINS HAS A DIRECT EFFECT ON HOW WE CONNECT WITH GOD.

to have a desire for God, yet they spend five hours a day in front of the TV, and five minutes with their Bible?

Now I'm not suggesting that you sit and read your Bible all day, but you should be cautious about what you spend your time doing. God wants us to be balanced physically, mentally, spiritually and socially. The brain is an interesting mechanism. If your days are filled with Reality TV shows and/or violent action movies full of obscenity and vulgarity, you're numbing yourself toward things of a Godly nature. I cringe every time I see a preview for a vampire, zombie movie, or movie with witchcraft and demons. Not because I'm scared but I know the effects that these movies can have on your brain and connection with God. Such entertainment pulls you away from the natural adoration you should have toward God. Most of these movies are a direct contradiction to our belief system, and are outright demonic! The Bible warns us to find whatever is good and holy, and think on these things.

Philippians 4:8 (NIV): Finally, brothers and sisters, whatever is true, whatever is noble, whatever is right, whatever is pure, whatever is lovely, whatever is admirable—if anything is excellent or praiseworthy—think about such things."

TRIALS DON'T STOP COMING BECAUSE WE'RE NOT READY.

Philippians makes it clear here that we are to flood our minds with pure things. It's been my experience that when I'm eating healthy and getting lots of protein, my strength in the gym goes through the roof. If I were to come off a weekend where I ate fast food and sweets, regardless of the strength I had the prior week, on Monday my body would feel weak and sluggish. I know how to do the workout and might be able to get through it but the process would be harder because my body wasn't conditioned for it. You see, what happens outside the gym has a tremendous effect on how you perform in the gym. In our spiritual lives, trials don't stop coming because we're not ready. The more physically, mentally and spiritually fit we are, the better we'll be able to handle the crosses we have to carry.

SOUL FOOD

A healthy spiritual diet is what I call foods for the soul. If I handed you a spiritual menu it would contain the following: Prayer, Worship, Bible-Study, Service, and Fasting. You'll need all of these things to get your mind prepared for whatever it is that God allows to come your way. When we're not feeding our brains healthy things we can be easily discouraged and distracted by the enemy. Performance during trials is what God wants to see. It's easy to praise the Lord when life is perfect, but a conditioned healthy

Christian will bless the Lord at all times. The question is will you be spiritually strong enough to do so? How healthy is your brain or, better yet, how healthy is your soul?

Isaiah 26:3 (NKJV): "You will keep him in perfect peace, whose mind is stayed on You, because he trusts in You."

In Matthew 6:1-18, Jesus gives us clear examples of what to do and what not to do in the areas of giving, fasting, and praying. Follow these principles for a great Spiritual Diet!

Prayer: Prayer is our lifeline to God. It keeps us in tune with God, who is the source of our strength. The most important thing about prayer is believing that God hears you and can answer your prayer in accordance with His will. Simply stated, keep it real with God. He knows the real you, so be real with Him. Prayer is most effective when you use your prayer time to also intercede on behalf of others.

Fasting: Fasting shows your dedication to God by your willingness to sacrifice and deny yourself. It also helps you clear your mind and detox your soul so that you can hear clearly from God. Fasting also helps you become disciplined for overcoming sin. After His baptism, Christ fasted for 40 days, and then He got the victory over the tempter. God will give you and me victory also. The question is how bad do we want it?

Worship: Worship to me is one of the most important things to add to your spiritual diet. The word of God says that God inhabits the praises of his people! This means God dwells within you. As God conditions you, you'll be at a place where you can worship in the midst of your situation because worship will be a way of life. It's hard to focus on problems and trials when you're focused on God. What the enemy tries to do is steal your worship of God. When you stress over your situation you are actually worshipping the devil by adopting that spirit of fear. That's why the Bible says in II Timothy 1:7 *"For God hath not given us the spirit of fear; but of power, and of love, and of a sound mind."*

Bible study: Bible study is a great way to learn more about God, but to also study past victories of God. The Bible is filled with stories of victories through Christ Jesus. The more we become familiar with the scriptures, the stronger our walk with him will be. I believe the Bible is a study guide to successful living. There are tons of versions and translations of the Bible out there, so I would suggest finding a Bible and a devotional that you can relate to and understand based upon where you are in your walk with God. It's also a good move to connect with other believers and search the scriptures together.

Service: Service is another way to worship God. You're actually worshipping God when you sacrifice your time for Him and His cause. Putting others before yourself is what Christ would do. Jesus lived a complete life of service. There's something special when we arrive at church with a spirit of giving and not taking. God does something to our soul when we offer our time, energy, and efforts to His glory. I believe that every Christian should be active in some sort of meaningful service, whether to your church or to your community. Christianity should be a lifestyle, not a title.

TRAINING

Let's look at athletes. They train during the off-season just for the upcoming season. We too, as Christians, should be ready for the upcoming season. Some of your seasons will bring you more hurt and pain than the season before. Our spiritual training goes far beyond what we endure. A huge part of our spiritual training is mastering the ability to successfully endure trails while keeping a good spirit about it.

What's your prayer life like? It's imperative that we, Christians, have a strong prayer life. When our prayer life is weak, we tend to struggle during the trials of life. Christians today would be able to handle the storms and trials of life better if they communicated more with God. He is the only One who can give them the power and peace of mind to overcome what they're going through. Far too often we wait until a trial or situation comes to pray to God. It would make more sense for us to have

GOD IS CALLING FOR US TO BE DISCIPLINED IN EVERY AREA OF OUR LIVES.

constant contact with our Savior beforehand, rather than waiting until a problem arises.

How often do we, Christians, cry out to God and say we want to get close to Him, yet our actions throughout the week say the exact opposite? How bizarre would it be if you left the gym after a great workout and ate a candy bar, potato chips and washed it down with a soda? All the sugar and calories will negate the effect of what you did in the gym.

The training we go through now is the testing ground used to prepare us for a time of trouble that's soon to come. God is calling for us to be disciplined in every area of our lives, to show ourselves worthy of the prize that awaits us in glory.

YOU ARE WHAT YOU EAT

Christians all over the world cry out to God and say they want to get close to Him, yet their actions throughout the week say the opposite. How unhealthy would it be if you left the gym after a great workout, then went and ate a candy bar, potato chips and washed it down with a soda? All of those sugars and calories will have the opposite effect on what you just did in the gym.

Jesus suggests that we feast on Him! He said, "I am the bread of life." He's the well that won't run dry! When we feast on God, by studying His word, fasting, praying and worshipping, it is then that we become most like Him. It only makes sense to embody the very power that's needed for this spiritual battle. I spent years fighting a spiritual battle without seeking help from God, and wondered why I continued to fail.

John 6:35 (NIV): "Then Jesus declared, "I am the bread of life. Whoever comes to me will never go hungry, and whoever believes in me will never be thirsty."

John 4:14 (NIV): "but whoever drinks the water I give them will never thirst. Indeed, the water I give them will become in them a spring of water welling up to eternal life."

{ WHEN WE FEAST ON JESUS, HE HAS A WAY OF CONSUMING US. }

The Bible makes it clear that if we are to be sustained through the trials of life, we need to be filled with the Spirit of God. Nothing else can take the pain away like our Jesus can. There isn't anything you can smoke or drink, and there's no pill you can take that will effectively and truly eliminate the pain. Alcohol and narcotics only temporarily mask the pain. When you sober up and the high comes down the emptiness is still there. When we feast on Jesus, He has a way of consuming us to the point that we are able to thrive through the pain. Jesus can and will take the pain away. What we, as Christians, must learn to do is discipline our brains to be in unison with God. There's a certain level of faith and trust that we must have in God.

Jesus won salvation for mankind because He was disciplined. Jesus had a constant communion with God. This made all the difference and it'll make the difference in your life. When Jesus rose from the dead, He told His disciples that He was leaving them but that He had a special gift for them. He went on to say that the gift of the Holy Spirit would be within them!

John 14:16-17 (NIV): "And I will ask the Father, and he will give you another advocate to help you and be with you forever the Spirit of truth. The world cannot accept him, because it neither sees him nor knows him. But you know him, for he lives with you and will be in you."

When you have the proper spiritual diet you're able to fully activate the Holy Spirit in your life. John said the world wouldn't accept the Spirit of God, but we, as disciples, will know Him because He lives in us. So ask yourself; does the Spirit of God live in you? Are you making your body a dwelling place where He can abide? There is so much power within you and me but we have to activate that power.

John 4:4 (NKJV): "You are of God, little children, and have overcome them, because He who is in you is greater than he who is in the world."

John is saying here that the God who's in you is greater than anyone or anything else. The problem is that the spirit of God that's in us is weakened due to the junk we put in our minds. God's effectiveness in our lives is competing with the many things we put in our minds. There will be a day when death will be no more; a day when the tears will dry up; a day when we'll have nothing but joy! Can you see the day?

Revelation 21:4 (NIV): "He will wipe every tear from their eyes. There will be no more death or mourning or crying or pain, for the old order of things has passed away."

Our spiritual state of mind has everything to do with how we'll handle the crosses that come our way. The pain is temporary, but the success is everlasting!

Micha's Workout Plan

Meet my friend Micha. Her strength & conditioning workout plan was quite interesting. Micha is a local radio host and personality, so on the radio and around town she's known as ML6. Micha's workout plan is refreshing yet challenging at the same time. I went to college with Micha and she has always been fun-loving and down to earth. If I can be completely honest with you, in my prodigal days, Micha would host my parties at the club. We both grew up in the church but we know that doesn't mean we had the church within us.

Now in her 30's, Micha began a real spiritual quest. It was prompted after a really bad car accident where she should have lost a leg but was spared. It was at that time that she began this intimate quest for God. Micha didn't want to just connect with God she wanted to know Him on an intimate and personal level. Her desire was to know God beyond what she had been taught and what was preached. She wanted to know who God was for her. After living the public, celebrity lifestyle for years, Micha felt convicted to make a change. She stopped drinking and started going to weekly Bible studies and church services on Friday evenings, Saturday and Sunday mornings. This was putting her in a positive place mentally and spiritually.

Micha has always taken her health seriously, and faithfully gets her annual check-ups. In May of 2013, Micha had her annual checkup and the results concerned her doctor. She felt something in her right breast and set up an appointment for a mammogram. The results showed that there was a 4-cm tumor in her right breast. Micha was diagnosed with stage 2 breast cancer. Once the doctor mentioned breast cancer, Micha tuned everything else out and just cried. The only thing she knew to do was call her pastor right away.

Her pastor tried to calm her down as she cried uncontrollably. Through the crying she was able to share the news of her being diagnosed with cancer. Her pastor simply said, "Micha feel how you feel, but don't lose your faith and stop crying." Her pastor knew the importance of keeping a cool head, and trusting God during times like these. Considering the journey Micha was about to embark upon, this was sound advice.

This news turned Micha's world upside down. How could she have cancer and why did she have cancer? She was on this spiritual journey and was getting so close to Christ, why now? Micha called her mother and father and broke the news to them. Her doctors assured her that they would be aggressive and immediately scheduled chemotherapy treatments for her. During one of her sessions, her doctors tried to figure out why she had breast cancer at such a young age. They had no explanation for it. Micha simply told them that they would never know why she got cancer, and that this was something between her and God!

Her first week of chemo was in the beginning of June. The week prior, four of her best friends from childhood came from Detroit to be with her. They covered her in prayer; praying over her mind, body and soul. You can imagine the comfort and encouragement that brought to her. Micha was known for her wild and funky hairstyles but she felt the weight of the cancer when her hair began to fall out after just one treatment. Discouraged, she called her pastor who encouraged her to not worry about her hair falling out because it was a sign that the chemo was working. Needing further encouragement, she called her dad who suggested that the barbershop be the next stop. Her dad encouraged her to embrace the journey by sporting the baldhead.

While Micha was in the barbershop she met an older man who asked her if she had cancer. When Micha told him she did, the guy strongly suggested that she share her story. This stranger wanted this very public figure to go public with her pain. Micha wondered how she could share something while she was still going through it. She noted his suggestion but was uneasy about making her cancer public. Her turn came up and the barber gave her a fresh smooth baldhead. I must admit, when I saw a picture of Micha on Instagram with her new look, I just thought she was pushing the envelope of style. It wasn't until I saw people say how they were praying for her that I realized she had cancer.

Days later Micha walked into a girl's conference and came across some young ladies who knew her. When they saw her baldhead they of course asked her, "Why did you cut your hair off?" With slight hesitation she told them she had cancer. The girls gasped in disbelief. Micha then assured the girls that she would be okay, and began to speak on the importance of being sure of yourself and self-esteem. After this empowerment speech she gave the young women, she saw how others where inspired by her strength, so she decided that she had cancer, but cancer didn't have her!

Micha decided it was time for action. She walked into the radio station, told her producers and staff that she was ready to share her journey with the world. That afternoon she took to the airwaves and disclosed to her listeners that she was in a fight with breast cancer, and then encouraged and ministered to her listeners. Instantly tons of calls and emails came in from fans showing support. Social media went crazy with people thanking her for being bold and sharing her story. This is when Micha found a ministry in her cancer. Women began to write her to tell her that they're no longer hiding under a wig, and that they're now empowered to fight back by embracing their baldhead. The emails and testimonies she heard from others encouraged her even more, which gave her the platform to share her faith.

If you ask Micha how she's doing today she'll tell you that she's happier than she's ever been. Her newfound relationship with God has gone to the next level. Micha now knows that the cancer not only aligned her with God and His will, but it put her in a position to serve and inspire others. Because of her popularity she does more in the community and speaks regularly. Does the chemo wear on her body? Yes. But God gives her strength.

The miracle behind this all is that half way through the chemotherapy, the tumor went from 4-cm to 1.5-cm. Next stop for Micha is surgery, more treatments and she'll be cancer free! Let her tell it, she's already healed it just hasn't manifested in the physical yet! Because of her spiritual diet, Micha's been able to carry her cross daily. Her connection to God prior to being diagnosed with cancer was a plan from God. God knew that she wouldn't stand a chance in her previous spiritual state, which is why He allowed things to come about when they did. Micha's experience with cancer has strengthened her faith in God and conditioned her for ministry!

Basic Training

1. What are the five things that you need in your spiritual diet?

2. What does Philippians 4:8 tell us to think of?

3. Why is it important to watch what you put in your brain?

4. What areas do you see God training you?

5. What does Jesus declare in John 6:35?

6. What areas can you change your spiritual diet?

7. What helped prepare Micha for the cancer?

8. What promise does Revelation 21:4 give?

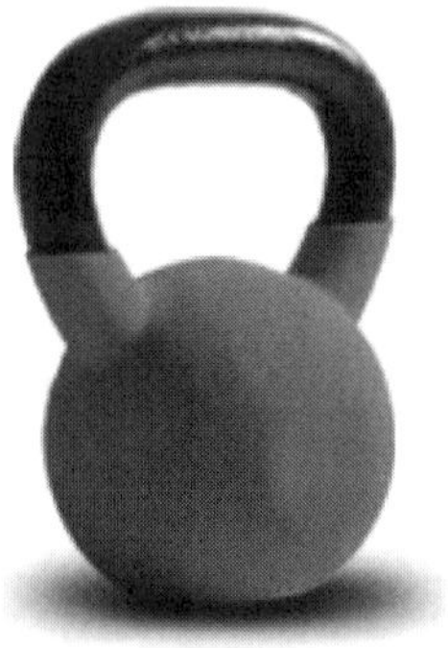

GROUP
TRAINING

GROUP TRAINING

Group Training

Chapter 1: The Gym Membership

Romans 8:17 NIV Now if we are children, then we are heirs—heirs of God and co-heirs with Christ, if indeed we share in his sufferings in order that we may also share in his glory.

John 14:1-2 NKJV "Let not your heart be troubled; you believe in God, believe also in me. In My Father's house are many mansions; if it were not so, I would have told you. I go to prepare a place for you."

1 Corinthians 12:12-14 NIV "Just as a body, though one, has many parts, but all its many parts form one body, so it is with Christ. For we were all baptized by one Spirit so as to form one body whether Jews or Gentiles, slave or free and we were all given the one Spirit to drink. Even so the body is not made up of one part but of many."

1 Peter 4:12-13 NIV "Dear friends, do not be surprised at the fiery ordeal that has come on you to test you, as though something strange were happening to you. But rejoice inasmuch as you participate in the sufferings of Christ, so that you may be overjoyed when his glory is revealed.

1 Peter 4:16 (NIV): "However, if you suffer as a Christian, do not be ashamed, but praise God that you bear that name."

Group Training

Chapter 1: The Gym Membership

ASK YOURSELF

1. Why should we view God's church as a fitness center?

2. How can someone be "in" God's church but not "of" God's church?

3. Why did Romans chapter 8 say we would share in Christ's sufferings?

4. Why does Peter tell us in 1st Peter chapter 4 to rejoice in sufferings?

5. What does Judas and many so-called Christians today have in common?

6. What if anything have you been selling God out for?

Group Training

Chapter 2: Your Personal Trainer

Romans 8:28 NIV "And we know that in all things God works for the good of those who love him, who have been called according to his purpose."

Romans 5:3-4 NIV "Not only so, but we also glory in our sufferings, because we know that suffering produces perseverance; perseverance, character; and character, hope.

Proverbs 3:5-6 NIV "Trust in the Lord with all your heart and lean not on your own understanding; in all your ways submit to him, and he will make your paths straight."

Jeremiah 29:11 NIV "For I know the plans I have for you," declares the Lord, "plans to prosper you and not to harm you, plans to give you hope and a future."

Chapter 2: Your Personal Trainer

ASK YOURSELF

1. Can you relate to Joseph's or Jon's story? If so, how?

2. Why does God use trials in our lives?

3. Based upon Romans 8, what advice could you give someone who is going through a rough time?

4. Ask yourself: Do you really believe in what Romans 8:28 says?

5. In Romans 5:3-4, why does Paul tell us to find glory in our sufferings?

6. How should we view our spiritual personal trainer?

7. What are the areas in your life where you feel like you could use a little spiritual strength training?

Group Training

Chapter 3: Trusting Your Trainer

John 16:33 NIV "I have told you these things, so that in me you may have peace. In this world you will have trouble. But take heart! I have overcome the world."

Hebrews 11:6 NIV "And without faith it is impossible to please God, because anyone who comes to him must believe that he exists and that he rewards those who earnestly seek him."

Isaiah 55:8-9 NIV "For my thoughts are not your thoughts, neither are your ways my ways," declares the Lord. "As the heavens are higher than the earth, so are my ways higher than your ways and my thoughts than your thoughts."

I Corinthians 10:13 NIV "No temptation has overtaken you except what is common to mankind. And God is faithful; he will not let you be tempted beyond what you can bear. But when you are tempted, he will also provide a way out so that you can endure it."

Group Training

Chapter 3: Trusting Your Trainer

ASK YOURSELF

1. What physical evidence does Christ have that shows us he's qualified to train us to be spiritually fit?

2. In John 16:33, Jesus tells His disciples that they'll go through hard times, but then He tells them to be of good cheer. Why is that?

3. Will God give you more than you can handle? If so, why?

4. Is faith what we have, or is faith what we practice?

5. Why did God ask Abraham to sacrifice his son?

6. Do you truly trust your trainer "God" with whatever happens in your life?

Group Training

Chapter 4: Weight Lifiting

I Timothy 4:7-8 NIV "Have nothing to do with godless myths and old wives' tales; rather, train yourself to be godly. For physical training is of some value, but godliness has value for all things, holding promise for both the present life and the life to come."

I Chronicles 16:11-12 NIV "Look to the Lord and his strength; seek his face always. Remember the wonders he has done, his miracles, and the judgments he pronounced,"

Matthew 11:28-30 NIV "Come to me, all you who are weary and burdened, and I will give you rest. Take my yoke upon you and learn from me, for I am gentle and humble in heart, and you will find rest for your souls. For my yoke is easy and my burden is light."

Matthew 27:32 NIV "As they were going out, they met a man from Cyrene, named Simon, and they forced him to carry the cross."

Job 1:8 NIV Then the LORD said to Satan, "Have you considered my servant Job? There is no one on earth like him; he is blameless and upright, a man who fears God and shuns evil."

Job 1:20-22 NIV "At this, Job got up and tore his robe and shaved his head. Then he fell to the ground in worship and said: "Naked I came from my mother's womb, and naked I will depart. The Lord gave and the Lord has taken away; may the name of the Lord be praised." In all this, Job did not sin by charging God with wrongdoing."

Job 2:9-10 NIV His wife said to him, "Are you still maintaining your integrity? Curse God and die!" He replied, "You are talking like a foolish woman. Shall we accept good from God, and not trouble?"

Matthew 5:45 NIV "He causes his sun to rise on the evil and the good, and sends rain on the righteous and the unrighteous."

Group Training

Chapter 4: Weight Lifiting

ASK YOURSELF

1. In 1st Timothy 4, what does Paul say is better than physical training?

2. What's the importance of having someone spot you while working out?

3. Who is your spiritual spotter?

4. Why did God allow Satan to afflict Job?

5. What was Job's response to losing everything?

6. At what point did Job experience his breakthrough and healing?

Group Training

Chapter 5: Cardio

Ezekiel 36:26 NIV "I will give you a new heart and put a new spirit in you; I will remove from you your heart of stone and give you a heart of flesh."

Hebrews 4:15-16 NIV "For we do not have a high priest who is unable to empathize with our weaknesses, but we have one who has been tempted in every way, just as we are—yet he did not sin. Let us then approach God's throne of grace with confidence, so that we may receive mercy and find grace to help us in our time of need."

Hebrews 12:1-3 NIV "Therefore, since we are surrounded by such a great cloud of witnesses, let us throw off everything that hinders and the sin that so easily entangles. And let us run with perseverance the race marked out for us, fixing our eyes on Jesus, the pioneer and perfecter of faith. For the joy set before him he endured the cross, scorning its shame, and sat down at the right hand of the throne of God. Consider him who endured such opposition from sinners, so that you will not grow weary and lose heart."

Isaiah 40:31 NIV "but those who hope in the Lord will renew their strength. They will soar on wings like eagles; they will run and not grow weary, they will walk and not be faint."

Psalms 34:18 NKJV "The Lord is near to those who have a broken heart, And saves such as have a contrite spirit.

Psalms 51:17 NIV My sacrifice, O God, is a broken spirit; a broken and contrite heart you, God, will not despise.

II Timothy 4:5 NIV "But you, keep your head in all situations, endure hardship, do the work of an evangelist, discharge all the duties of your ministry."

Revelations 12:11 KJV "And they overcame him by the blood of the Lamb, and by the word of their testimony"

Group Training

Chapter 5: Cardio

ASK YOURSELF

1. What does Paul say in Hebrews about God understanding our pain?
2. Why is it so important to have a heart like Jesus?
3. What does Isaiah say about stamina?
4. Why did Paul write that letter to Timothy?
5. What does Psalms say about a broken heart and contrite spirit?
6. What training are you learning from your present trial?
7. Who has God placed in your life for you to help spiritually train?
8. How can you begin to implement these training techniques into your everyday activity or life?

Group Training

Chapter 6: Burning Fat

Ephesians 5:15-17 NIV "Be very careful, then, how you live—not as unwise but as wise, making the most of every opportunity, because the days are evil. Therefore do not be foolish, but understand what the Lord's will is."

Jonah 2:9-10 NIV "But I, with shouts of grateful praise, will sacrifice to you. What I have vowed I will make good. I will say, 'Salvation comes from the Lord. And the Lord commanded the fish, and it vomited Jonah onto dry land."

Hebrews 12:5-6 NIV "And have you completely forgotten this word of encouragement that addresses you as a father addresses his son? It says, "My son, do not make light of the Lord's discipline, and do not lose heart when he rebukes you, because the Lord disciplines the one he loves, and he chastens everyone he accepts as his son."

Hebrews 12:7-9 NIV "Endure hardship as discipline; God is treating you as his children. For what children are not disciplined by their father? If you are not disciplined—and everyone undergoes discipline—then you are not legitimate, not true sons and daughters at all. Moreover, we have all had human fathers who disciplined us and we respected them for it. How much more should we submit to the Father of spirits and live!"

Hebrews 12:10-11 NIV "They disciplined us for a little while as they thought best; but God disciplines us for our good, in order that we may share in his holiness. No discipline seems pleasant at the time, but painful. Later on, however, it produces a harvest of righteousness and peace for those who have been trained by it."

Psalms 51:10 NIV "Create in me a pure heart, O God, and renew a steadfast spirit within me."

Group Training

Chapter 6: Burning Fat

ASK YOURSELF

1. What fat "sins" in your life does God want to burn away so you can be fit for Him?

2. What was the main reason Jonah wanted to avoid going to Nineveh?

3. What fears do you have that's stopping you from fulfilling your purpose in life?

4. What did God use to save Jonah's life?

5. What reason did Hebrews chapter 12 give for God disciplining His children?

6. How do Jonah's and Jason's attitude compare with your attitude during your training? What can you focus on to help with your attitude? Jonah 2:9-10 & Hebrews 12:7

7. What life predicament, restriction and/or trial is God using to trim or burn the fat off you?

Group Training

Chapter 7: Diet

Philippians 4:8 (NIV): Finally, brothers and sisters, whatever is true, whatever is noble, whatever is right, whatever is pure, whatever is lovely, whatever is admirable—if anything is excellent or praiseworthy—think about such things."

Isaiah 26:3 (NKJV): "You will keep him in perfect peace, whose mind is stayed on You, because he trusts in You."

II Timothy 1:7 "For God hath not given us the spirit of fear; but of power, and of love, and of a sound mind."

John 6:35 (NIV): "Then Jesus declared, "I am the bread of life. Whoever comes to me will never go hungry, and whoever believes in me will never be thirsty."

John 4:14 (NIV): "but whoever drinks the water I give them will never thirst. Indeed, the water I give them will become in them a spring of water welling up to eternal life."

John 14:16-17 (NIV): "And I will ask the Father, and he will give you another advocate to help you and be with you forever the Spirit of truth. The world cannot accept him, because it neither sees him nor knows him. But you know him, for he lives with you and will be in you."

John 4:4 (NKJV): "You are of God, little children, and have overcome them, because He who is in you is greater than he who is in the world."

Revelation 21:4 (NIV): "He will wipe every tear from their eyes. There will be no more death' or mourning or crying or pain, for the old order of things has passed away."

Group Training

Chapter 7: Diet

ASK YOURSELF

1. What are the five things that you need in your spiritual diet?
2. What does Philippians 4:8 tell us to think of?
3. Why is it important to watch what you put in your brain?
4. What areas do you see God training you?
5. What does Jesus declare in John 6:35?
6. What areas can you change your spiritual diet?
7. What helped prepare Micha for the cancer?
8. What promise does Revelation 21:4 give?

ABOUT THE AUTHOR

JEREMY J. ANDERSON

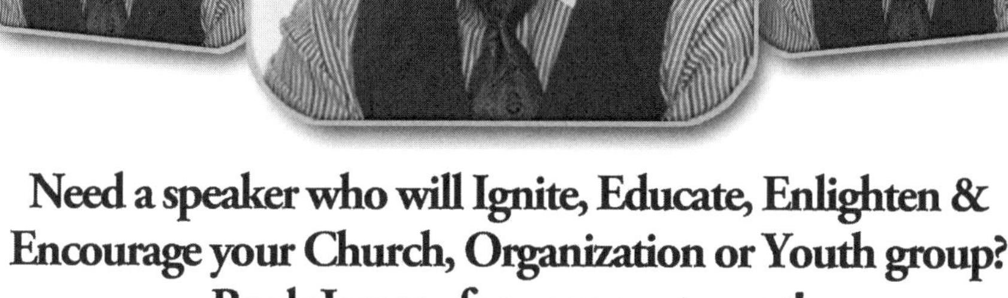

Need a speaker who will Ignite, Educate, Enlighten & Encourage your Church, Organization or Youth group? Book Jeremy for your next event!

For booking or more information contact 256.759.7492
or email j.j.anderson80@gmail.com.
Visit the website www.jeremyanderson.org!
: @256Jeremy
YouTube : Jeremyanderson1000

Daily you'll receive:
*Motivational Messages
*Daily Devotionals
*Inspirational Video
*Recorded Sermons
* & so much more!

Keep up with Jeremy daily by downloading his Free App!

"JeremyDaily"

Order Volume 1 of the *Modern Disciple Series* "Self-Destruction"

THE MODERN DISCIPLE SERIES *Volume 1*

SELF-DESTRUCTION

how to die of **self** and live in the **Spirit** of God.

JEREMY J. ANDERSON

THIS WAS THE BOOK THAT STARTED IT ALL!

Join Jeremy on a journey to Self-Destruction as we seek to die of ourselves, so that we can live in the Spirit of God.

• Available Now •

www.JeremyAnderson.org

Also available on eBook:

A Division of Spirit Reign Communications